How Ireland is Governed

How Ireland is Governed

James D. O'Donnell

INSTITUTE OF PUBLIC ADMINISTRATION
DUBLIN

© Institute of Public Administration 1979

ISBN 0 902173 87 1

Published by
Institute of Public Administration
59 Lansdowne Road
Dublin 4 Ireland

First Published 1965
Second Edition 1966
Third Edition 1967
Fourth Edition 1968
Fifth Edition 1974
Sixth Edition 1979

Set in 11 on 12 point Baskerville and printed by Mount Salus Press, Dublin

Contents

Preface to the Sixth Edition

In the fourteen years since this book first appeared there has been a notable advance in the amount of material on public organisations available to students and the general reader — indeed the Institute of Public Administration has played a big part in bringing this about. However the need for a book that provides a simple clear description of the whole system of government in Ireland subsists.

How Ireland is Governed is largely based on the specialised monographs published by the Institute and I am greatly indebted to the various authors for allowing me to make use of their work. A large number of public servants and officers from bodies outside the public service helped with additional material and clarified numerous points for me. I thank them for their patience and goodwill.

I am particularly grateful to my colleagues in the Institute and friends in the public service for help in revising parts of the text for this edition.

James O'Donnell
May, 1979

1. The People

Irish governments derive their power from the people. Ireland, therefore, is a democracy — a word meaning 'rule by the people' derived from the two Greek* words 'demos' (people) and 'kratein' (to rule). Most governments nowadays would claim to be democratic.

In the past, few governments were democratic. Rulers derived power from immemorial custom, from the actual power and wealth they commanded or from religious laws. The forms of government to be found were monarchies (kingships) or autocracies (dictatorships) or oligarchies ('rule by the few', e.g. a government conducted by a council of aristocrats) or theocracies ('rule by God', e.g. government conducted by a priestly caste).

In modern times the American and French revolutions undermined immemorial custom as a source of authority by providing a popular alternative. The French revolutionaries, moreover, by executing a king who claimed authority not only from immemorial custom but also from God (through the principle of the divine right of kings), gravely weakened religion as a plausible source of governmental authority. Thus the people and force now remain as the two obvious sources of authority. Naturally, most governments go out of their way to claim that they are democratic rather than tyrannical.

'Democracy' is not an exact term because people use it in different senses. In the Greek city-states the people came together in one place and voted on public issues. They made their deci-

---

*Many of the basic concepts we use in talking about systems of government are based on Greek words because the ancient Greeks were the first people to develop a body of literature dealing with these topics.

1

sions by a majority. Such democracy is called *direct demo-cracy*. Modern states are too big to make direct democracy possible. Instead of deciding issues for themselves people elect representatives to act on their behalf. Such indirect democracy is called *representative democracy*. Since all the non-democratic forms of government aim to restrict power and in-fluence to a minority within the state they necessarily deny freedom and political equality to most citizens. The ideas of freedom and equality have, therefore, become closely associated with democracy. However, in a state where everything was settled by majority vote the majority could well become tyrants. To promote freedom and equality therefore, most democracies pass laws which guarantee basic rights to all citizens. Such democracies are called *liberal or constitutional democracies*. Moreover, because the actual degree of freedom and equality enjoyed by a citizen is related to his income and education, many people believe that democracies should aim to bring about a society where every citizen is broadly equal to his fellows in these respects. States which have laws to bring such a condition about are known as *social democracies*.

Ireland is a representative democracy. It is a liberal democracy. It has also many laws aimed at taking some wealth from the rich through taxation in order to provide for the less well off; and it has many citizens who would describe themselves as social democrats. However, it also has many citizens who believe that within the scope provided by a liberal constitution each citizen should be as free as possible to use his energy, skills and enterprise in the pursuit of wealth. Such people oppose the tendency towards social democracy. In the spectrum of political allegiance their views would be regarded as right-wing or conservative.

Because 'democracy' means so many different things people sometimes get involved in protracted and confusing argument about whether a particular country is democratic or not. The fact is that some governments elected by a majority of the people act in an extremely authoritarian manner. It is much more sensible to think of democracy as a quality that exists to varying degrees in different countries at different times.

Whatever view one takes of the degree to which democratic values should be pursued in society, one must accept that there is a certain amount of knowledge that every citizen must have if democracy is to exist at all. Citizens must understand how power is transferred from the people to the government, what controls the people have on the exercise of that power and what organisations exist to enable the government to use the power delegated to them to achieve national development which is the aim of government. The Chapters that follow seek to provide that knowledge.

2. The Constitution

When a new state emerges — by revolution or colonial with-drawal — one of its first tasks is to draw up and adopt a constitution. The primary function of a political constitution is to state the supreme laws by which the country will be governed, i.e. it must state the basic laws that will govern the legislature (parliament), the executive (government) and the judiciary (the legal system). Many constitutions, however, are more than legal documents. They include a description of the objectives the state will strive for and an enunciation of the rights of the individual. These give constitutions an emotional appeal and strengthen peoples' reverence for them. Constitutions are adopted by the people directly by referendum or indirectly through their elected representatives. Changes in the constitu-tion are effected again either directly or indirectly as laid down in the constitution itself. Constitutions serve as a check on government: they govern government. If a citizen, for example, feels his constitutional rights are infringed by a law, he can bring the case before the Supreme Court and if the law is declared repugnant to the constitution, it ceases to exist. Conversely constitutions enhance the authority of government.

The Constitution of Dáil Éireann

The Sinn Féin candidates elected at the general election of December 1918 who were not 'on the run' or imprisoned, met in Dublin in January 1919 and constituted themselves as Dáil Éireann. They drafted a constitution in Irish. This constitution dealt with the authority of the Dáil, the appointment and authority of a príomh-airech (literally a 'first minister' but who in English came to be called 'president') and of a government, the appointment of a chairman of the Dáil and finally the pro-vision and audit of funds.

The Dáil chose its president and confirmed his choice of ministers. Ministers had to be members of the Dáil, were answerable to the Dáil and could be dismissed by the Dáil. There was no monarch or president outside or above the Dáil to symbolise the state. At this time, the Dáil also drew up a Declaration of Independence and a Democratic Programme which expanded on what was contained in the Proclamation of the Irish Republic, 1916. In Irish constitutional history it is with the Constitution of Dáil Éireann that the new state began.

The Government of Ireland Act, 1920

This Act, passed by the British Parliament at Westminster, proposed to set up two parliaments, two administrations and two judicial systems, one for most of Ulster, the other for the rest of Ireland. In effect it offered home rule and partition. It did envisage, though, the eventual appearance of common political organs. The only part of the Act that was implemented was that dealing with Northern Ireland.

The Constitution of the Irish Free State

The struggle for independence ended with the Treaty of 1922. The British Government insisted on partition along with Commonwealth status. The Treaty and the Constitution of the Irish Free State were ratified by the Constituent Assembly (Dáil) which had been returned in the elections of 1922.

Provisions

Under the constitution the Irish Free State had its own legislature (Dáil and Senate), its own executive (Executive Council), and its own judiciary. The constitution provided for Dominion status within the British Commonwealth, that is, the British monarch was formally head of state. However, the nationalists had fought for a republic and notwithstanding its acceptance of Commonwealth status, the constitution was given a strong republican tone. The Constituent Assembly asserted that 'the undoubted right' it had to enact the constitution came 'from God to the people'. In addition, Article 2 of the constitution declared that 'all powers of government, and all authority legislative, executive and judicial in Ireland, are derived from the people of Ireland'.

The constitution of Dáil Éireann had concentrated power in the Dáil (it would be impracticable for a revolutionary government to try to rule in close consultation with the people), but provisions in the Constitution of the Irish Free State were intended to make parliament and the government as responsive as possible to the wishes of the people. Apart from proportional representation and judicial review of the constitution there were provisions for referendum and for the initiation of legislative proposals by those outside parliament. A declaration of rights that included freedom of expression, freedom to practise religion, freedom of association, habeas corpus and the inviolability of the citizen's home further strengthened the citizen's position vis-à-vis the government and parliament.

As in other dominions, the British monarch had a representative in Ireland, a governor-general. The constitution, and declarations elicited mainly by the Irish representatives at subsequent Commonwealth meetings (and most notably embodied in the Statute of Westminster, 1931), ensured that his functions were purely formal. Members of parliament were obliged to take an oath of allegiance to the Crown.

When Mr de Valera came to power in 1932, he promoted legislation to remove the symbols and procedures of the Commonwealth. The oath and the governor-generalship were abolished. Finally in 1937 Mr de Valera proposed a new constitution—Bunreacht na hÉireann.

Bunreacht na hÉireann
'In the Name of the Most Holy Trinity, from Whom is all authority and to Whom, as our final end, all actions both of men and States must be referred,

We, the people of Éire,

Humbly acknowledging all our obligations to our Divine Lord, Jesus Christ, Who sustained our fathers through centuries of trial,

Gratefully remembering their heroic and unremitting struggle to regain the rightful independence of our Nation,

And seeking to promote the common good, with due observance of Prudence, Justice and Charity, so that the dignity and freedom of the individual may be assured, true social order attained, the unity of our country restored, and concord

established with other nations,
   Do hereby adopt, enact, and give to ourselves this Consti-
tution'.

The preamble to Bunreacht na hÉireann asserted once more the right of the people to make their own constitution. Article 2 of Bunreacht na hÉireann declares that the national territory 'consists of the whole island of Ireland, its islands and the territorial seas'. Article 3, recognising the existing situation, declares that 'pending the reintegration of the national territory', the Oireachtas shall have the same area of jurisdiction as that of Saorstát Éireann. Article 4 declares that 'the name of the State is Éire or in the English language, Ireland' and Article 5 adds 'Ireland is a sovereign, independent, democratic state'.

Bunreacht na hÉireann made provision for a President who would act not only as ceremonial head of state, but also as the guardian of the people's rights and of the Constitution. It provided for a Dáil and a Seanad and a cabinet government headed by a Taoiseach (prime minister). Justice was to be administered 'in courts established by law, by judges appointed in the manner provided by this Constitution' — and under the Constitution all judges are appointed by the President on the advice of the government.

The provisions for proportional representation, the referendum and judicial review of the Constitution were retained. Personal rights were again guaranteed.

Having been approved by the Dáil, Bunreacht na hÉireann was proposed to the people in a referendum and adopted by them.

The EEC Treaties

Under the Constitution no international agreement may become part of the domestic law of the state save as may be determined by the Oireachtas. When Ireland approached the issue of joining the European Communities it found that it would have to sign treaties which conferred on the EEC institutions powers to make certain laws directly binding on Irish people. Since this was not allowed under the Constitution, the Constitution had to be amended before Ireland could join. Accordingly the Third Amendment of the Constitution Act, agreed to in a referendum in 1972, provided that no actions needed to give effect to Community measures could be invalidated by reason of unconstitutionality. When Ireland signed the EEC Treaties and became a member, the Treaties, which are in effect the constitution of the EEC, became superior to the Irish Constitution.

3. The President

Under Bunreacht na hÉireann, the President is elected by the direct vote of the people. Every citizen over thirty-five years of age is eligible for the office. A former or retiring President may become a candidate on his own nomination. Other candidates must be nominated by at least twenty persons each of whom is a member of one of the Houses of the Oireachtas or by the councils of at least four county councils (including county boroughs). The persons or bodies that may nominate candidates can subscribe to one candidature only. If only one candidate is nominated for the office of the President, there is no need to proceed to a ballot for his election. If a member of either House of the Oireachtas is elected, he vacates his seat in that House.

On his inauguration the President takes the following oath before the members of the Oireachtas, the judges of the Supreme Court and the High Court and 'other public personages': 'In the presence of Almighty God I ... do solemnly and sincerely promise and declare that I will maintain the Constitution of Ireland and uphold its laws, that I will fulfil my duties faithfully and conscientiously in accordance with the Constitution and the law, and that I will dedicate my abilities to the service and welfare of the people of Ireland. May God direct and sustain me.'

The electorate is the same as that for Dáil elections. The President's term of office is seven years. He can be re-elected once only. His official residence is Áras an Uachtaráin (formerly the Viceregal Lodge) in the Phoenix Park, Dublin. During his term of office, the President may not leave the country unless the government consent.

A president or monarch is a head of state, i.e. a person who in the performance of certain official acts symbolises the state.

In some countries the president (e.g. in the USA) is also chief executive, i.e. head of the government. The President of Ireland is head of state only; the Taoiseach is chief executive.

The President normally acts on the advice and authority of the government. On the nomination of Dáil Éireann he appoints the Taoiseach. On the advice of the Taoiseach and with the prior approval of Dáil Éireann, he appoints members of the government and presents them with their seals of office. On the advice of the Taoiseach, he accepts the resignation or terminates the appointment of a member of the government. The Oireachtas is summoned by the President and normally dissolved by him on the advice of the Taoiseach.

Before a Bill becomes law, it must have the President's signature. The President promulgates the law by having a notice published in *Iris Oifigiúil* (the official gazette), stating that the Bill has become law. The supreme command of the defence forces is vested in the President. Commissioned officers in the defence forces hold their commissions from him.

The Republic of Ireland Act, 1948, assigned all executive powers in connection with international affairs to the President acting on the advice of the government; so it is to the President that foreign ambassadors present their credentials and it is the President who, on the advice of the government, accredits Irish representatives abroad. It is the duty of the Taoiseach to keep the President generally informed on matters of international as well as domestic policy. On the advice of the government, the President can commute the sentences of criminal offenders.

Bunreacht na hÉireann, however, envisages the President as more than a ceremonial head of state; it gives him certain powers that make him the guardian of the Constitution. First, the President may, after consultation with the Council of State, refer any Bill to the Supreme Court for a decision as to whether it contains anything repugnant to the Constitution. Since any amendment of the Constitution requires approval at a referendum, a government which insisted on a particular provision that had been declared repugnant would have to submit it to the people. Secondly, if a majority of the Seanad and not less than one-third of the Dáil petition him to decline to sign a Bill on the ground that 'it contains a proposal of such national importance that the will of the people thereon ought to be ascertained' the President may accede to the request after consultation with the Council of State and sign only when the proposal has been approved by the people in a referendum or by a new Dáil after a dissolution and a general election. Thirdly, to cover an emergency, the President has power to convene a meeting of either or both Houses of the Oireachtas. Again, the President must consult the Council of State before exercising this third discretionary power. The Council of State is composed of the Taoiseach, the Tánaiste (deputy Taoiseach), the Chief Justice, the President of the High Court, the Chairman of Dáil Éireann (an Ceann Comhairle), the Chairman of Seanad Éireann, the Attorney General, every person able and willing to act who has held office as President, Taoiseach, or Chief Justice and any other persons (to a total of seven) whom the President may appoint at his own discretion. The President need not necessarily follow the advice of the Council.

The President has one power which he may exercise at his absolute discretion. If the Taoiseach fails to retain the support of the majority in the Dáil, he will ask the President to dissolve the Dáil and then 'go to the people'. In this case, the President can refuse, thus forcing the Taoiseach to resign and giving the Dáil the opportunity to nominate a successor. No President has used this power so far and it is not known in what circumstances it might be used. One could speculate that the President would use his power to prevent a series of costly general elections in a period of instability or in a case where the Taoiseach lost the support of his own party on a personal rather than a public issue.

There is no vice-president of Ireland. If the President dies during his term of office, or is incapacitated, or is abroad, or is removed from office or fails to carry out functions enjoined on him by the Constitution, the Constitution provides for a Commission to act in his place. The Commission would consist of the Chief Justice, the Chairman of Dáil Éireann and the Chairman of Seanad Éireann. The Commission may act by any two of their number.

The President, as the symbol of the state, is accorded ceremonial honours on public occasions. He has an aide-de-camp. As first citizen, the President takes precedence over all others, even visitors, however distinguished. He has his own standard which, along with the national flag, flies over Áras an Uachtaráin, when he is in residence, and, when appropriate, at other places where he is present. The presidential standard consists of a golden harp on a blue ground.

The President has in his custody the presidential seal. This seal may be affixed only to documents made by him and only by his direction, and its use must be authenticated by his signature. The seal is in the form of a circle approximately 15 cms (6 inches) in diameter with a harp in the centre and the name of the State in Irish, *Éire*, beneath it; a ring of Celtic ornamentation surrounds both. The harp is a reproduction of the Brian Boru harp in Trinity College, Dublin, and the ornamentation is reproduced from the base of the Ardagh chalice.

Apart from its place in the government of the country, the Presidency is an effective instrument in spreading goodwill abroad. The President sends messages to other heads of state — greetings on national feast-days, condolences in the event of national tragedies; he receives distinguished visitors from abroad; answers or re-directs foreign enquiries. On occasion the President will represent Ireland abroad. The President also uses his office to lend prestige to important cultural activities within the state.

To help him in his work the President has a small secretariat.

The office of the President in its present form was introduced under Bunreacht na hÉireann. Presidents elected since 1937 have been Dr Douglas Hyde (1938-45), Seán T. Ó Ceallaigh (1945-59), Eamon de Valera (1959-73), Erskine Childers (1973-74), Cearbhall Ó Dálaigh (1974-76), and Patrick J. Hillery (1976 —).

4. The Houses of the Oireachtas

The Constitution provides that the Oireachtas (national parliament) shall consist of 'the President and two Houses, viz.: a House of Representatives to be called Dáil Éireann and a Senate to be called Seanad Éireann.'

Dáil Éireann has 148 members called Teachtaí Dála (TDs). They are returned by the 42 constituencies into which the country is divided; twenty-six constituencies return three members each, ten return four, and the remaining six, five. Each member of the Dáil represents about 20,000 people. The constituencies are revised by the Oireachtas at least once in every twelve years to take account of changes in the distribution of the population.

Seanad Éireann has sixty members. Eleven are nominated directly by the Taoiseach, three are elected by the National University of Ireland, three by the University of Dublin, and the remaining forty-three are elected from five panels of candidates—the Cultural and Educational Panel, the Agricultural Panel, the Labour Panel, the Industrial and Commercial Panel, the Administrative Panel. Each panel contains the names of persons with knowledge and practical experience of the interests represented by the panel.

Eligibility

Every citizen who has reached the age of twenty-one years and who is of sound mind and not serving a heavy prison sentence is eligible for membership of the Dáil and Senate, except the President of Ireland, the Comptroller and Auditor General, judges, members of the defence or police forces on full pay, and civil servants. A member of the board of a state-sponsored body must resign on becoming a member. No person may be at the same time a member of both Houses.

Nomination of Candidates

A candidate for Dáil Éireann may nominate himself or, if he wishes, be nominated by a registered voter in the constituency which he wishes to represent. The candidate may indicate on his nomination paper the political party he represents; if he intends to stand as an independent he may describe himself as 'non-party'. At the election those particulars will appear on the ballot papers. A candidate for panel election to the Senate may be nominated by four members of the Houses of the Oireachtas or by a registered nominating body (e.g. the Association of Secondary Teachers, Ireland, which is on the Cultural and Educational Panel). A member of either House may not join in the nomination of more than one person. At an election for university members candidates are nominated by two registered electors of the university as proposer and seconder, and by eight other electors as assenting to the nomination.

The Electorate

For Dáil elections every citizen who has reached the age of eighteen years and is not disqualified by law (e.g. is not serving a prison sentence for treason or felony) has the right under the Constitution to vote at elections.

The voting is by secret ballot. Postal voting is confined to members of the Garda Síochána and full-time members of the defence forces. Members are elected on the system of proportional representation by means of the single transferable vote.

The electorate for the forty-three members of the Seanad elected from panels of candidates consists of the members of the Dáil, the members of the Senate and the members of every council of a county or county borough. Where a person is a member of the electorate by virtue of more than one qualification his name is entered once only in the electoral roll. There is a separate election for each panel. The electorate for the six members elected from the Universities consists of every citizen who has received a degree (other than an honorary one) from those universities and has attained the age of twenty-one years. Every election of the members of the Seanad is held on the system of proportional representation and by secret postal ballot.

The Election System
   Election is the act by which the people delegate their authority. Naturally there are strict regulations to ensure that this
important function is not abused. Great care is taken to ensure
that the register of voters is accurate and that each elector votes
once only. The secret ballot prevents intimidation. Bribery,
etc. of electors is penalised.
   There are many different election systems, each with its own
advantages and disadvantages. Under the system used in the
UK the country is divided into one-member constituencies.
The elector votes by placing a cross, X, against the name of the
candidate he prefers. The candidate with the most crosses wins
the seat. It is said that this procedure favours the two-party
system; in discouraging smaller parties it reduces voter choice.
Since the strongest party is likely to get a far greater number of
seats than its proportion of the votes would seem to warrant,
people say the system makes for greater stability of government.
   Under the system used here, the state is divided, as we have
seen, into constituencies returning three or more members
each. The elector can indicate his own order of preference
amongst the candidates whose names are on the ballot-paper
by putting the figure 1 against the name of his first choice, a 2
against that of his second choice, a 3 against his third choice
and so on. A voter supporting one of the larger parties normally finds more than one candidate of that party standing in his
constituency and so he can use his vote to secure the election of
the best of them, from his point of view.
   The ballot paper you get when you come to vote looks some-
thing like the diagram on page 16.

Counting the Votes
   Votes are counted by the quota system. In a three-member
constituency a member who received one-third of the first
preference votes would clearly be entitled to election. But he
would not need even that. If four candidates divided the votes
equally between them, each would receive exactly one quarter
and there would be none left over. But suppose that three
candidates each receive just a vote or two more than a quarter
of the total then any other candidate must receive less than a

Counterfoil No..............	Marcáil órd do rogha sna spáis seo síos. Mark order of preference in spaces below.	Marc Oifigiúil Official Mark
		DOYLE—WORKERS' PARTY (James Doyle, of 10 High Street, Builder).
		LYNCH—DEMOCRATS (Jane Ellen Lynch, of 12 Main Street, Grocer).
		O BRIAIN—CUMANN NA SAORANACH (Seamus O Briain, ó 10 An tSráid Ard, Oide Scoile).
		O'BRIEN, EAMON (Barrister)—NON-PARTY (Eamon O'Brien, of 22 Wellclose Place, Barrister).
		O'BRIEN, EAMON (Solicitor)—YOUNG IRELAND. (Eamon O'Brien, of 102 Eaton Brae, Ranelagh, Solicitor).
		O'CONNOR—NATIONAL LEAGUE (Charles O'Connor, of 7 Green Street, Publican).
		THOMPSON—FARMERS PARTY (William Henry Thompson, of Dereen Park, Farmer).

TREORACHA

I. Féach chuige go bhfuil an marc oifigiúil ar an bpáipear.

II. Scríobh an figiúr 1 le hais ainm an chéad iarrthóra is rogha leat, an figiúr 2 le hais do dhara rogha agus mar sin de.

III. Fill an páipear ionas nach bhfeicfear do vóta. Taispeáin *cúl an pháipeir* don oifigeach ceannais, agus cuir sa bhosca ballóide é.

INSTRUCTIONS

I. See that the official mark is on the paper.

II. Write 1 beside the name of the candidate of your first choice, 2 beside your second choice, and so on.

III. Fold the paper to conceal your vote. Show the *back of the paper* to the presiding officer and put it in the ballot box.

quarter. So the quota in a three-member constituency is fixed not at one-third of the total vote but at the next whole number above one-fourth. For clearly if three candidates each receive such a quota, then between them they have secured more than three-fourths of the total and no other candidate can possibly equal their score. Similarly if four deputies are to be elected, then any candidate who polls more than a fifth of the votes — by however small a margin — is entitled to be elected. In a constituency returning n deputies we can express the quota as the smallest whole number that exceeds the figure we obtain when we divide the total number of valid votes cast in that constituency by $(n + 1)$. In a three-member constituency where the total number of valid votes cast is 24,733, one quarter of the total valid vote is $6183\frac{1}{4}$ and so the quota is 6184.

In an election a popular candidate may get more than the quota. His surplus votes — say 5,000 — are then distributed according to the second preference. This is done by examining all his votes — say 15,000 — and recording the number of second preferences for each of the other candidates; since only the surplus 5,000 votes have to be distributed, the number of second preferences for each candidate is multiplied by 5,000 and divided by 15,000.

If candidates have still not reached the quota to fill the remaining seats, the candidate with the lowest number of votes is eliminated and his original votes distributed according to the second preferences and any votes received by him on another candidate's second preferences are distributed according to the third preferences. If a candidate now reaches the quota, he is elected. Any surplus he has is re-distributed. The process of eliminating the candidate with the lowest number of votes is continued until all the seats are filled. The table on page 18 shows the election results and transfer of votes in a constituency in the general election of 1977.

The system of proportional representation, which was introduced to Ireland by the Government of Ireland Act, 1920, and which is prescribed by our Constitution, gives a wider choice of candidates to the elector than the UK system. It also gives representation to a wider range of opinions. Another advantage to the electorate is that it forces deputies to 'nurse' their constituencies carefully for in this duty they have to face the

ELECTION RESULTS AND TRANSFER OF VOTES (1977)

Constituency of Sligo-Leitrim

TOTAL ELECTORATE 45,418
VALID POLL 35,651
NUMBER OF SEATS 3
QUOTA 8,913

NAMES OF CANDIDATES	First Count	Second Count		Third Count		Fourth Count		Fifth Count	
	Votes	Transfer of MacSharry's Surplus	Result	Transfer of Higgins' Votes	Result	Transfer of Bree's Votes	Result	Transfer of McManus' Votes	Result
BREE, DECLAN	1,282	+ 59	1,341	+ 164	1,505	− 1,505	—	—	—
GALLAGHER, JAMES (F.F.)	6,152	+ 1,486	7,638	+ 72	7,710	+ 295	8,005	+ 1,055	9,060
*GILHAWLEY, EUGENE (F.G.)	7,988	+ 118	8,106	+ 273	8,379	+ 165	8,544	+ 480	9,024
HIGGINS, TOMMY (Lab.)	1,074	+ 45	1,119	− 1,119	—	—	—	—	—
*McLOUGHLIN, JOSEPH (F.G.)	5,786	+ 134	5,920	+ 311	6,231	+ 226	6,457	+ 1,032	7,489
McMANUS, SEÁN	2,399	+ 215	2,614	+ 263	2,877	+ 549	3,426	− 3,426	—
*MacSHARRY, RAY (F.F.)	10,970	− 2,057	8,913	—	8,913	—	8,913	—	8,913
NON-TRANSFERABLE PAPERS NOT EFFECTIVE	—	—	—	+ 36	36	+ 270	306	+ 859	1,165
TOTAL	35,651	—	35,651	—	35,651	—	35,651	—	35,651

Names of Candidates Elected:— MacSHARRY, RAY (F.F.)
GALLAGHER, JAMES (F.F.)

*Sitting member

rivalry of the other deputies in their constituency—whether these belong to an opposition party or their own.

A disadvantage of the system is that it may lead to instability of government. It is difficult for a party to achieve an overall majority—half the number of seats plus one—not to say a runaway victory. A number of general elections in the past have been indecisive and have had to be closely followed by other elections before a single party gained an overall majority. At other times, power to make or break a government has rested in the hands of independent deputies. (People sometimes put too much stress on this last point. After all someone voted in wants to stay in; he or she is loath to risk seat and deposit in unnecessary elections; and of course there is the expense of it all. These factors weigh even more heavily with Independents who have not the backing of party funds. Independents then, who find themselves holding the balance of power are much more constrained than an abstract consideration of the situation would suggest.) All in all, Irish experience suggests that the argument that the system leads to instability does not hold.

Duration, Dissolution, Membership of the Houses

Five years has been fixed by law as the maximum term of life of the Dáil. A presidential proclamation sets out the date of dissolution of the outgoing Dáil and the date on which the new Dáil will meet. A general election for members of the Dáil must take place not later than thirty days after the dissolution and the newly elected Dáil must meet within thirty days from the polling date. The Minister for the Environment appoints the date of the poll.

The elections are set in motion by the Clerk of the Dáil who issues a writ or form to the returning officer in each constituency (the sheriff or county registrar), directing him to cause an election to be held in his constituency. When the count is completed the returning officer endorses on the writ the names of the members returned for the constituency and forwards it to the Clerk of the Dáil. A newly elected member is notified by the Clerk to attend and sign the roll of members. At the first meeting of the House after the election, the Clerk announces the names of all members returned to serve in it.

The outgoing Ceann Comhairle is deemed to be elected to the new Dáil without any actual election, unless, of course, he wishes to retire.

Attendance in the House is not compulsory. Deputies tend to specialise in particular areas of government and this limits their interest in legislation. They have, besides, a heavy load of constituency work.

If a member is suspended from the Dáil for disregarding the authority of the Chair, his suspension on the first occasion continues until the fourth day, on the second occasion until the eighth day and on the third or any subsequent occasion until the twelfth day of sitting after the day of his suspension. The suspension may be lifted if the member submits to the House a written expression of regret.

A general election for the Seanad takes place not later than ninety days after a dissolution of Dáil Éireann. The first meeting of the new Seanad takes place on a day fixed by the President on the advice of the Taoiseach. The Minister for the Environment issues orders within seven days of the dissolution of the Dáil, setting out the dates and times of the elections of the panel and university members. The returning officer for the panel elections is the Clerk of the Seanad. For the National University it is the Vice-Chancellor and for Dublin University it is the Provost.

Attendance in Seanad Éireann is not compulsory either. TDs are paid (from 1 March 1978) £6,775 a year and Senators £3,988. Certain office-holders are paid additional sums. The Taoiseach receives £11,867 in addition, the Tánaiste £8,730, ministers £7,942, and ministers of state £5,105; the Ceann Comhairle receives in addition £7,942, the Leas-Ceann Comhairle £4,018, the Cathaoirleach of the Seanad £3,379 and the Leas-Cathaoirleach £1,807. In addition allowances for expenses are made to the leaders of qualified parties in the Dáil. For instance, if there were one party in government (as at present) that allowance would be £19,809. Where two qualified parties are in office, the allowance for the leader of the larger one is £13,866 and that for the leader of the smaller one is £5,943. If there is one non-government qualified party the allowance for its leader is £49,533. If there are two non-government qualified parties, the allowance for the leader of the larger one is £34,672 and that for the leader of the smaller one is £14,861.

The payment of public representatives ensures to some extent that one need not be wealthy to engage full-time in politics.

Privileges of Members

Under the Constitution, the members of each House of the Oireachtas are privileged from arrest in going to, returning from, and while in the precincts of, either House unless guilty of treason, felony or a breach of the peace. What they say in either House, even when published, is subject only to the rules of the House itself, not to a court or any other authority. Each House has power to ensure freedom of debate and to protect itself and its members in the exercise of their duties.

The Powers of the Houses

Since the Seanad derives from a restricted electoral college, its role is the minor one. This is the status of the upper house in most countries that are not federal states. In most federal states, e.g. the USA, the Federal Republic of Germany, Switzerland, each of the two Houses has special powers in particular areas of government which put them on an equal footing.

To take an example: in the USA the House of Representatives has the sole power of impeachment and the sole right to initiate legislation on revenue, while the Senate has the sole right to confirm or reject presidential appointments and concur in treaties.

Under our Constitution the government are responsible to the Dáil alone. When the government are appointed, the Dáil has the right to examine and criticise their administration; it is the Dáil that in effect passes all money Bills, i.e. Bills that concern finance only, because the Seanad has power only to delay their enactment for twenty-one days; and in regard to other Bills to which the Seanad does not agree within the ninety days it has to consider them, they may be deemed to be passed by both Houses if the Dáil passes a resolution to that effect. It may be said that essentially the Seanad acts as an advisory body to the Dáil.

Legislation

To carry out its work and to implement its policies the government needs the authority of the Oireachtas. It presents its proposals in the form of Bills. The Houses of the Oireachtas debate Bills, amend them and finally vote on them. The Houses devote most of their time to the public Bills presented to them by the government. A private member of the Dáil may also introduce a public Bill (other than a money Bill). We might note that there are also private Bills, i.e. Bills promoted for the particular interest or benefit of any person or locality as distinct from measures of public policy. Like private members' Bills they form a very small part of the work of the Oireachtas.

Public Bills—they are mainly initiated in the Dáil—go through five stages.

First stage

In either House any member may move for leave to introduce a Bill and if leave is given the order is made for its second reading and the Bill is printed and circulated to members. In the Dáil a member of the government or a minister of state or, in certain circumstances, a private member may present a Bill without previously obtaining the leave of the House, and the Bill is printed and circulated. Subsequently, an Order is made by the Dáil for its second reading. The first stage arises only in the initiating House; in the other House the Bill is first considered on second stage. A government Bill is introduced in the Dáil by a minister or minister of state. In the Seanad a government Bill is introduced by the Leader of the House (a senator who supports the government).

Second stage

This is the stage at which the general principles of the legislation are debated. The important speeches are usually made at this time. The Bill may be rejected. Normally, however, improvements in the Bill are suggested in general terms, the second reading is agreed to and the Bill is ordered to be considered in committee (third) stage.

Third (committee) stage

The committee is usually the whole House. A highly technical Bill may be referred to a select or special committee. In this third stage the Bill is considered in great detail. Each section and each amendment is discussed carefully and passed or defeated separately.

Fourth (report) stage
The Bill coming from committee stage is tidied up. Amendments accepted are incorporated.

Fifth (final) stage
The Bill is finally considered before it is passed.

A Bill amended by the Seanad is sent back to the Dáil for its agreement.

When a Bill, other than a Bill to amend the Constitution, is passed or deemed to be passed by both Houses, it is sent to the President for his signature and promulgation as law. The President signs the Bill not earlier than the fifth day and not later than the seventh day after the date on which the Bill is presented to him, unless a motion requesting his earlier signature is agreed to by the Seanad, or unless he decides to refer it to the Supreme Court or to a referendum. A Bill to amend the Constitution passed or deemed to be passed by both Houses and approved at a referendum is signed forthwith by the President. The signed copy is kept in the offices of the Supreme Court.

Statutory Instruments
The Houses of the Oireachtas create new legislation and reform the old. Modern legislation is complex and the Houses of the Oireachtas would be clogged with unfinished business if they had to go into the minutiae of, say, road traffic legislation. So they empower ministers to promulgate Statutory Instruments, i.e. rules and regulations that have the force of law. A select committee of the Seanad examines Statutory Instruments to ensure that this delegated law-making power is sensibly and properly used.

The Oireachtas and State Finance
The Dáil votes the money the government need to keep go-

ing their supply of services to the people (current expenditure) and also the money they need to spend in any year to help the country to create more wealth (capital expenditure).

The state's financial year begins on 1 January. About the beginning of the year the government presents to the Dáil the Estimates for Public Services, a substantial volume that gives detailed information of the estimates on the supply services. The discussion on the various items in these estimates continues in the Dáil for months and when agreement has been reached on all the amounts to be allotted, an Appropriation Bill is passed which authorises the expenditure. Because of the state's growing involvement in the economic life of the country there is a tendency for the financial commitments of the state to grow continuously. That in turn tends to demand an increasing amount of discussion in the Dáil on the estimates. However, while all this discussion is taking place the departments need to be able to continue providing their various services. Under the Central Fund (Permanent Provisions) Act, 1965, each department can spend up to four-fifths of its previous year's estimate pending passage of its current estimate. This allows debates in the Dáil on the estimates to be extended over virtually the whole of the current financial year.

In January of each year the Estimates of Receipts and Expenditure are presented to the Dáil. These show in a concise form

(1) how much was spent and how much was received in the past year;

(2) how much it is expected will be spent in the coming year, and

(3) how much it is expected will be received in the coming year,

basing the estimate on tax rates in force. A few days later comes the budget. The budget is a statement by the Minister for Finance in which he reviews the economic state of the country and outlines his proposals for expenditure — current and capital — and taxation for the current year. If new taxation is involved he indicates the services or commodities on which he proposes to impose the tax and/or the increase of the rate of direct tax, e.g. income tax. Temporary authority for any tax increases is given, pending the enactment of the Finance Bill, in the following July.

There is in practice no separate Dáil debate on the capital budget. The tax proposals in the current budget attract most of the attention. Yet the capital budget, which sets out in some detail projected capital expenditure for the coming financial year together with projected resources, has an immense impact on economic development through its effect on the availability of credit.

Having voted public money, the members of the Dáil must be in a position to know that the money has been spent on the items they intended it to be spent on. From its own members the Dáil appoints a Committee of Public Accounts at the beginning of each financial year. This committee is usually twelve in number. No minister or minister of state serves on it. Its chairman is traditionally a member of the opposition. It is the Committee of Public Accounts that examines the report of the Comptroller and Auditor General on the past year's accounts. The Comptroller and Auditor General is appointed by the President on the nomination of the Dáil to control all payments out of the Central Fund and to audit all accounts dealing with money voted by the Oireachtas. In addition, the Committee of Public Accounts examines the accounting officers of departments, i.e. the permanent heads of departments and major offices. It then draws up its report for the year and presents it to the Dáil.

The Oireachtas and EEC Legislation

When Ireland joined the European Communities in 1973 it bound itself to abide by certain rules and regulations made by the various EEC institutions. Subsequently the Oireachtas established the Joint Committee of the Houses of the Oireachtas on the Secondary Legislation of the European Communities. It consists of eighteen TDs and eight senators. It has power to examine and report to both Houses on drafts of Community legislation, on acts of the Community institutions, on regulations made under the European Community Act 1972, and on other statutory instruments made in Ireland in consequence of Irish membership of the Community.

The Oireachtas and state-sponsored bodies

In 1978 the Oireachtas established a Joint Committee on

State-Sponsored Bodies consisting of seven TDs and four senators. Its function is to examine the reports, accounts and overall operational results of a number of state-sponsored bodies engaged in trading or commercial activities.

Sittings and Business of the Houses

The Dáil sits for about 80 days in the year and the Seanad for about 30. The Dáil sits on Tuesdays at 2.30 p.m. and on Wednesdays and Thursdays at 10.30 a.m. On Tuesdays and Wednesdays it adjourns not later than 9.00 p.m. and on Thursdays not later than 5.30 p.m. The hours vary depending on the state of business in the House.

For every sitting there is a printed Order Paper. Drawn up under the direction of the Ceann Comhairle, it sets forth the business the Dáil will conduct that day. The bulk of the time is allotted to public business. The Taoiseach has the right to determine each day the order in which government business is to be taken. A small amount of time is allotted to private business (private Bills and matters relating to them) and to questions. Parliamentary questions are submitted in writing to the appropriate department three days in advance. They are put down to elicit information on the work of departments and they are the principal way in which the Dáil can keep a check on administration. Answers to questions may be given orally by a minister or minister of state or they may be printed in the official report. Questions cannot lead to a debate or decision by way of vote but deputies dissatisfied with an answer can be allotted half an hour in which to have the matter discussed when the House is adjourning for the day.

The Seanad meets on Wednesdays and Thursdays and occasionally on Fridays. Its sittings are largely dependent on the volume of business sent to it from the Dáil. Since it is a smaller body than the Dáil, its discussions are shorter. Private Bills are introduced in the Seanad.

Chairmen of Houses

The Ceann Comhairle of Dáil Éireann and the Cathaoirleach of Seanad Éireann have charge of the conduct of proceedings and the general administration of their Houses. They take no part in debate. They preside over sittings and are the sole judges of order. The debates in each House are published under the supervision of the chairmen and so are the journals which contain daily records of the decisions of the Houses. Each House elects its own chairman and deputy chairman. Each chairman represents his House in all its external relations.

Officials

The office of the Houses of the Oireachtas, which is staffed by civil servants, carries out the secretarial work of the Houses under the direction of the Clerk of the Dáil and the Clerk of the Seanad respectively. The office of the Houses of the Oireachtas prepares the Order Paper and Journal of Proceedings of each House and the official report of debates in each House. It has custody of all records and other documents belonging to the Houses. It makes all the arrangements necessary to facilitate deputies and senators in their parliamentary work.

Location

Dáil Éireann and Seanad Éireann both meet in Leinster House, Dublin.

5. The Government

According to the Constitution the government shall consist of not less than seven or more than fifteen members. The Taoiseach, the Tánaiste (deputy prime minister) and the Minister for Finance must be members of the Dáil. The other members of the government must be members of the Dáil or Seanad but not more than two may be members of the Seanad. The government are responsible to the Dáil alone. Ministers have the right, however, to attend and be heard in each House of the Oireachtas.

Usually each member of the government heads one of the departments of state into which the central administration is organised, but occasionally a minister heads more than one department. Each of these departments conducts a segment of the state's business and is composed of civil servants. The government act as a body and are collectively responsible to the Dáil for their conduct of the state's affairs. When the Taoiseach resigns all the other members of the government must resign also.

Besides the members of the government proper, there are other political office holders who, while they are not actually members of the government, hold office subject to the same general conditions. First, there are the ministers of state who assist their ministers in their parliamentary and departmental work. The maximum number of ministers of state is fixed by law at ten. They are appointed by the government. Secondly, there is the Attorney General who, though he cannot be formally a member of the government, is 'the adviser of the government in matters of law and legal opinion' and represents the state in legal proceedings. He need not be a member of the Oireachtas and in practice he seldom is.

The government consist of men who are leading figures of the party or the coalition of parties which has a majority in the Dáil, and more particularly, leaders of that important group within the party, 'the parliamentary party', that is, the representatives of the party elected to the Dáil or Seanad. If the members of the government are drawn from one party, they are well-known to each other and to the party. They are therefore to some extent a ready-made team. Their views and efforts will have had an important part in forming the party's outlook and programme. If the government consists of a newly-formed coalition they will not have the experience of working together —though necessity should soon weld them into a team. In either case, the fact that the government as a whole are collectively responsible for the departments of state administered by the individual ministers is a powerful unifying force.

In a formal sense it is true that, as the Constitution says, 'the sole and exclusive power of making laws for the State is ... vested in the Oireachtas'. But what happens in practice is that the members of the party or coalition of parties that have won the general election leave the formulation of policy to their leaders, now the government, and by giving them their support in the Oireachtas secure the implementation of these policies. Thus it is the government who decide what measures will be introduced, when and for how long they will be debated, what will be voted upon and what conceded; and it is the members of the government who assume the task of conducting business through the Dáil. In matters of finance, the government's initiative is exclusive, for Article 17 of the Constitution states that 'Dáil Éireann shall not pass any vote or resolution, and no law shall be enacted, for the appropriation of revenue or other public moneys unless the purpose of the appropriation shall have been recommended to Dáil Éireann by a message from the Government signed by the Taoiseach'. In dealing with money Bills, the Dáil may decrease the proposed expenditure but it may not increase it.

The Taoiseach

The Taoiseach or head of the government is appointed by the President on the nomination of the Dáil. In practice it is usually the people who nominate the Taoiseach because in general elections, owing to the party system, the people realise that they are voting for leaders and governments as well as for the local candidates for whom they indicate their preference on the ballot paper. The Taoiseach nominates the other members of the government for appointment by the President with the previous approval of the Dáil. He assigns each member of the government to a particular department (this allocation of departments does not need to be approved by the Dáil). He appoints one member of the government to be Tánaiste who acts in his place if he becomes incapacitated. The Taoiseach nominates the Attorney General to the President, who is bound to appoint his nominee. Curiously enough the appointment and dismissal of ministers of state is a function of the government as a whole. The Taoiseach may advise the President to accept the resignation of a member of the government. He may request a member to resign, and, should the member 'fail to comply with the request, his appointment shall be terminated by the President if the Taoiseach so advises'. If at any time the Taoiseach resigns, 'the other members of the Government shall be deemed also to have resigned from office'. The Taoiseach nominates eleven of the sixty members of the Seanad and advises the President of the day for the first meeting of the Seanad after a general election for that House. He may, as and when he thinks it necessary, 'cause to be prepared under his supervision a text (in both the official languages) of (the) Constitution'.

The Taoiseach is the central co-ordinating figure who takes an interest in the work of all departments, the figure to whom ministers naturally turn for advice and guidance when faced with problems involving questions of broad policy or of special difficulty. He attends the regular meetings of heads of state or of government of the European Community, which deal with major issues of Community policy. His leadership is essential to the successful working of the government as a team. He initiates major debates in the Dáil, on the adjournment or otherwise, and answers questions in the Dáil where the attitude of the government towards important matters of policy is involved.

The office of Taoiseach is characterised by the personality of the man holding it and the political situation in which he finds himself. Much depends on whether he, effectively controls his cabinet or not, whether he initiates policies or allows his ministers always to do so; whether he interferes in some (or all) sectors or leaves his colleagues alone.

The government and the people

The government meet twice a week in Government Buildings, Merrion Street, Dublin. At these meetings decisions are made which can vitally affect the country's prosperity. There is no doubt that great power rests in the hands of the government. When one sees how government legislation passes inexorably through the Houses of the Oireachtas, one might wonder if this power is not too great. It is well then to consider some of the practical restraints on the government.

First, the government and legislature can act only within the terms of the Constitution* and of the country's international obligations, of which those imposed by membership of the European Communities are perhaps the most important. Disputes as to whether particular policies or acts are in conformity with these obligations are settled by the Irish or Community courts, whose decisions are binding. These obligations are powerful constraints on the dictatorial attitude towards the use of power which has been epitomised in the often quoted remark by the Emperor Tiberius: 'Oderint dum metuant' — 'Let them hate me so long as they fear me'. Moreover, democratic government simply cannot afford such disdain of the popular will: its power is derived from party power which in turn is derived from popular support. In making policy decisions the government will be swayed by the opinions of its supporters in parliament (who knows what argumentation and bargaining take place behind closed doors before a policy that has the unanimous support of the party is formulated!); by the opinions of groups and associations throughout the country; by an assessment of how the people in general will react. Having decided on legislation the government must be in a position to execute it, for the execution of policy is the basic function of government. For success in this the co-operation of the people

---

*However, in a national emergency the Constitution allows the Oireachtas to pass legislation that in normal circumstances would be repugnant to it.

who will be affected is necessary and those who will administer the policy must feel that it is practicable as well as reasonable.

Democratic governments rule largely by persuasion. As politicians, the members of the government must seek to please their supporters, who are usually concerned with local and short-term conditions; as statesmen they must take a long-term view of the country's needs. In practice they may compromise to reconcile what are often contradictory demands.

We might note here the importance of the press and television in the political life of a country. Newspapers, magazines, books and television inform the citizens on public affairs by reporting parliamentary debates, speeches, demonstrations and government activity. They analyse political, social and economic problems and praise or criticise government policy in the light of such analyses. The fact that there are many newspapers reflecting many different interests ensures that public matters are discussed from most points of view. Thus the citizen's understanding of national problems is deepened and he has a good basis on which to assess the government's administration. In short, the press enables the citizen to supervise the government's use of the power he and his fellow-citizens have delegated to it.

Government policies

The function of government is to take such action as the general good of the community requires. One can discover five strands in the government's work. In looking after justice, defence and external affairs the government are preserving *order*. They promote *economic development* through their interest in finance, industry and commerce, agriculture, transport and power, posts and telegraphs and the state-sponsored bodies devoted to or assisting in production. They care for the nation's *welfare* by providing health services, social insurance and social assistance, and local government services. *Culture*, too, is within their ambit: the government support and largely direct education, provide library services, museums, art galleries, etc., aid the national theatre, language revival societies and many other cultural activities. Finally the government concern themselves with the organisation and smooth running of the *administrative machinery* through which they themselves work — the civil service and other government agencies.

Broadly speaking, the government must submit their proposals to the Dáil in the form of Bills before they can act. These proposals reflect the government's policies. Governments derive their basic policies from the theory of government they and their parties subscribe to. Thus since the capitalist and communist theories of government are diametrically opposed, the basic policies of a western democratic country will differ from those of, say, Red China. Given this primary division there are still further differences caused by the varying views of people on the degree of government intervention needed to achieve the common good. In a western country one may find a party on the right (conservative) which holds that the less governments intervene in the lives of the people the better, and a party on the left (socialist) which holds that in a modern state only extensive government action can secure the happiness of the majority; and in between those extremes, groups varying in their attitudes from left to right.

The Constitution of Ireland is politically of the centre: on the one hand it guarantees the citizen's right to private property and on the other hand it pledges the state to take special care of the weaker sections of the community. Irish political parties tend to preserve this balance in their constitutions, and so there are only marginal doctrinaire differences between them.

Practical reality too directs our politicians to the centre. People in the Republic are not seriously divided on racial, religious or economic issues so that cardinal points of difference upon which political dissidents can converge do not exist. Militating against strong socialism are the facts that a very high proportion of all houses and agricultural land in the country is occupied by the people who own them, that there is no great store of wealth which can be readily re-distributed and that to increase the gross national product (the total value of the goods and services produced each year) taxation must be low enough to encourage private investors and people with valuable skills, technical and managerial, to invest their money and their talents in Ireland. Militating against extreme conservatism has been the history of the country and the fact that as industry grows the workers in the towns press for better social services.

Irish governments, then, tend to be pragmatic. Where the political parties differ are on priorities, e.g. here and now should the old age pensioners be given more and education less? Should agriculture be given increased aid? And so on.

Department of the Taoiseach

The Taoiseach's department acts as secretariat to the government and provides a briefing and co-ordinating service for the Taoiseach in relation to his work as head of government, both at home and abroad. An office attached to it, the Government Information Services, issues government pronouncements and handles public inquiries. Another office, the Central Statistics Office, is also attached to this department. It collects census, trade and other statistics which are a valuable guide in policy-making.

6. The Civil Service

The scope of government is so great that it is impossible for ministers and members of the Oireachtas to look after every detail themselves. That is where the civil servant comes in. A civil servant is a member of the staff appointed to help a minister to carry out his functions, to advise him on various points of administration and to ensure that decisions and laws are properly and fairly applied. All the civil servants of all the departments collectively form what is called the civil service.

Departments

There are 18 departments: the Department of the Taoiseach; Finance; Public Service; Health; Social Welfare; Fisheries; Tourism and Transport; Posts and Telegraphs; Agriculture; Industry, Commerce and Energy; Defence; Justice; Foreign Affairs; Environment; Labour; Gaeltacht; Education; Economic Planning and Development. Attached to some departments there are offices which are self-contained and largely independent of the parent department. These include the Valuation Office, the Civil Service Commission, the Office of the Revenue Commissioners, the Office of Public Works, which are attached to the Department of Finance; the Forest and Wildlife Service which is attached to the Department of Fisheries; the Land Commission, which is attached to the Department of Agriculture. A number of these offices are larger than some full departments.

There are about 50,000 civil servants (this figure does not include industrial civil servants, mainly tradesmen and craftsmen, of whom there are about 7,300). The Department of Posts and Telegraphs is by far the largest department. It employs about 23,000 people all of whom are classed as civil servants.

Grades

There are over 1,000 grades of employment in the civil service. The number in each grade may vary from several thousand to a single individual. The grades fall into two main divisions — *general service* and *departmental*.

The general service grades form the core of the civil service and it is from them that the popular image of the civil service derives. There are about 15,300 people in them. The main general service grades, in descending level, together with the numbers serving in each on 2 January 1978 are:

Secretary (19), Deputy Secretary (15), Assistant Secretary (79), Principal Officer (266), Assistant Principal Officer (609), Administrative Officer (121), Higher Executive Officer (1,049), Executive Officer (1,623), Staff Officer (831), Clerical Officer (3,070), Clerical Assistant (7,699).

The Clerical Class consisting of supervisory Staff Officers, Clerical Officers and Clerical Assistants is the largest class in the general service grades. It handles the less complicated correspondence and accounts, copying, addressing, indexing, form filling, typing, tabulating, etc.

The Executive Class, the next largest class, comprises Higher Executive Officers and Executive Officers. Officers in these grades help in putting into operation policies and decisions made by the Oireachtas, their own minister and their own superior officers. It is also part of their work to resolve complexities and difficulties arising out of the operation of such policies and decisions.

The Administrative Class is the smallest one in the general service. It consists of Administrative Officers, Assistant Principals, Principals, Assistant Secretaries, Secretaries. This class organises and directs the work of departments, handles the major difficulties which arise in carrying out existing policy, advises ministers in the formulation of new policies and generally assists ministers in their parliamentary and statutory work. The junior grade in this class, that of Administrative Officer is, broadly speaking, a training grade.

The Secretary of a department is its permanent head. The minister, though superior to the Secretary, is its temporary head because his term of office expires with that of the government of which he is a member.

Most civil servants serve in departmental grades. The main distinction between general service grades and departmental grades is that those in the general service grades may be moved from one department to another while those in departmental grades are normally recruited for service in one department only, the particular grade being instituted because of the needs of the particular department. The departmental grades include all sorts of specialist staff, professional and technical — engineers, architects, doctors, lawyers, meteorologists, postal sorters, postmen, draughtsmen, accountants, seed analysts, veterinary surgeons, clerks of works, laboratory assistants, minor technicians. They vary in status from the equivalent of Secretary of a department to subordinate level. The main group in the departmental grades is engaged on work for which the specialised knowledge and training of the members equip them. The members of some departmental classes receive their training within the civil service, e.g. tax officials, customs and excise officers, social welfare officers. As in the general service grades, there are open competitions to departmental grades and promotion is mainly to higher grades in the same class of work.

The headquarters of all the civil service departments are in Dublin but several have local offices throughout the country. Civil servants may be asked to serve anywhere in the state, but most of the general service classes and many of the departmental classes serve in Dublin.

General Functions

Some civil servants help the government to provide services directly to the people — one thinks of postal services, children's allowances, housing grants, advisory services for farmers. Some provide funds for and give central direction to large categories of people who are themselves providing services to the community — teachers, the Garda Síochána, the defence forces. Some have liaison with local government and the state-sponsored bodies that also supply the nation with a number of varied services. Some are concerned with ensuring through on-the-spot inspection or examination of accounts or holding tribunals that the laws governing large areas of the nation's life are being fairly applied — laws governing the professions, business, industry, the courts. Some are concerned with the planning that is needed to ensure that the country can produce more and more wealth. Some are concerned with gathering the money the government needs to carry out its work — customs and excise officials and income tax officials. Some are concerned to ensure that Ireland plays its proper role in international affairs — notably, of course, in the work of the institutions of the European Communities.

The Oireachtas and the civil service

Parliamentary questions enable the Oireachtas to keep aspects of the general work of the civil service under review. Moreover, deputies and senators are constantly in direct touch with ministers and departments through deputations, personal interviews and correspondence on matters ranging from important policy issues to representations on behalf of individual constituents. The work of civil servants is therefore under close scrutiny and naturally they take care not only that they deal fairly with the public but also that they can be seen to have done so. The close interest taken by the Oireachtas in the work of the civil service is extremely important in our democracy. In fulfilling this duty civil servants are involved in much paper-work and constrained by fairly rigid rules. This means that they have not the same freedom in the despatch of business as an ordinary commercial firm.

Restrictions on civil servants

It is desirable that in a democracy every citizen should play an active part in public affairs. It is also desirable that the political impartiality of the civil service — its ability to serve every government elected by the people with equal effectiveness — be maintained. Certain restrictions are placed on civil servants in order to find a balance between those principles.

Civil servants have full freedom of private political expression, including voting rights in parliamentary and local elections, but no civil servant may stand for election to the Dáil or Seanad. About 80 per cent of civil servants are free to engage in politics. Civil servants engaged in the framing of policy proposals — broadly speaking, executive officers and higher grades — are barred from such activity.

The Official Secrets Act prohibits unauthorised communication of official information; breaches of the Act are punishable by fine or imprisonment. While civil servants may take on other work outside official hours, they are expected to ensure that there is no conflict between their outside activities and their official duties, e.g. an officer would be precluded from doing outside work for a firm which does business with his department.

Co-ordination

The work the public service carries out is diverse and inter-related. To reduce the possibility of confusion of purpose between the various bodies that comprise the public service special measures are taken to achieve co-ordination over large and important areas.

Thus the work of the local authorities is largely co-ordinated by the Department of the Environment, the work of the regional health boards is co-ordinated by the Department of Health and each state-sponsored body acts under the aegis of one or other of the departments. Four departments — the Departments of the Taoiseach, Finance, Public Service, and Economic Planning and Development — have a co-ordinating role in regard to particular aspects of the work of all the other departments.

The Department of the Taoiseach co-ordinates the legislative programme of the government, which is the aggregate of all the Bills being drawn up within departments for presentation to the Oireachtas, and all matters submitted for decision to the regular meetings of the government. The Department of Finance co-ordinates the financial demands being made by the various departments. The Department of the Public Service co-ordinates the structural changes made in the public service and the recruitment, remuneration and development of public service personnel. The Department of Economic Planning and Development co-ordinates the planning for development that goes on in the other departments. Co-ordination between departments that have a common interest in a particular activity is often sought through the use of inter-departmental committees.

The civil service and the government

People who correspond with departments of state are familiar with the opening form of replies — 'I am directed by the Minister for — — — — to inform you that . . .'. The volume of public business is so great that only a fraction of it comes directly to the attention of ministers. Civil servants become adept in applying ministerial policies to particular cases so that it might be said that their decisions are the ones ministers would arrive at if they had the full facts before them. The formula cited above points to an important principle — the principle of ministerial responsibility. The minister is responsible for the work of his department. In view of this responsibility, civil servants who are a minister's agents, must take care that decisions they make reflect the minister's views, not their own proclivities.

The principle of ministerial responsibility is a safeguard against bureaucracy — the situation that would arise if nearly all decisions on public business were made by civil servants on their own authority without responsibility to the Dáil through a minister. Since civil servants are bound to secrecy, ministers are traditionally expected to defend them from unfair public criticism.

Civil Service Commission

The vast majority of civil servants are selected for appointment by the Civil Service Commission who conduct competitions. The competitions consist of one or more of the following types of test — written examination, oral examination, interview, practical examination — or any other appropriate tests. The Commissioners, in consultation with the Department concerned and the Department of the Public Service, draw up the regulations regarding the necessary qualifications, age, health and so on, for the various appointments. The Commission is concerned with the recruitment of school-leavers and the recruitment of people with professional or technical qualifications, or prescribed experience. In addition, the Commission holds competitions for persons already in the civil service who apply for posts higher than those they already hold. A small number of appointments, e.g. Secretaries of Departments, are made directly by the government.

The work of the civil service

The Ministers and Secretaries Act, 1924, and later amendments gives the allocation of work between the departments. Outlines of the work of departments are given in Appendix A.

The Devlin Report

Modern government is big business. Moreover it is an expanding business basically because people demand that the state provide more and more economic, social and cultural services. This calls for the employment of more people to provide those services. It also calls for an expanding economy to provide the extra money to pay for them. So modern governments find themselves deeply concerned in creating the conditions in which the economy can expand. That calls for further expansion of the public service.

It is clearly of crucial importance to the country's well-being that the public service be so organised and staffed that it can carry out its work as efficiently as possible within the general constraint of public accountability.

In 1966 the Minister for Finance, Mr Jack Lynch, appointed a group of people with wide experience of the public service and private business to examine the organisation of the public service. The group, whose chairman was Dr Liam St. J. Devlin, reported in 1969. Their main recommendations were as follows:

1. Separation of policy and execution: There are two basic aspects to the work of government — as indeed of any business — (1) deciding on what should be done (policy) and (2) doing it (execution). At present our departments are relatively large because they carry out both functions. This in itself is not a problem. However, what tends to happen is that execution completely overshadows policy formulation. Everybody in a department right up to the Secretary is overwhelmed by decisions that have to be made about the day-to-day work. Engrossed in immediate issues, departments often fail to discern problems looming on the horizon and therefore fail to formulate policies to deal with them in time. To obviate this weakness the group recommended that the typical department should consist of the Aireacht — the central core of the department grouped around the minister

and responsible for policy formulation and general direction and control — and satellite bodies responsible for policy execution. These would be of two kinds — executive offices to carry out executive work now being done by departments and executive agencies which would mainly be the present non-commercial state-sponsored bodies.

2. A new public service department: The new department would report to the Minister for Finance and the Public Service. It would look after the general organisation of the public service, its personnel and the provision of the materials and equipment it needs to carry out its work. These matters are a concern of all the organisations within the public service. By building up a body of top experts in each of them, the Public Service Department would also be in a position to provide a high-grade consultancy service to the whole public service.

3. Staff units: Every body of work must be planned and financed, and there must be a proper organisation to do it and the right staff to man the organisation. Omit any of these things and the work either will not be done at all or if it is it will be done inefficiently. The group therefore recommended that four staff units be set up in each department one each for planning, finance, organisation and personnel.

4. Commissioner for administrative justice: At present the system whereby a citizen can appeal against decisions affecting him made by the public service is underdeveloped. The group recommended that a Commissioner for Administrative Justice be appointed who would set up an appeals system throughout the public service.

5. Integration of the service: The group recommended that the distinction between general service and departmental grades be abolished so that every public servant would be able to move about in the public service in pursuing his career.

6. Promotion: The group recommended that promotion to every post of Assistant Principal and higher should be open to every qualified officer and that every post should be filled by the best officer available.

7. Changes in existing departments: The group recommended a redistribution of functions among departments. It

recommended the abolition of the Board of Works and the creation of a new Department of National Culture.

Government response to Devlin
The new Department of the Public Service was established in November 1973. Shortly afterwards the Minister for the Public Service (who is also Minister for Finance) set up a Public Service Advisory Council to monitor progress on the reorganisation of the public service and to report annually to each House of the Oireachtas.

The pace of reform is slow. The government now aims to press ahead with the establishment of the four staff units (planning, finance, personnel and organisation) in each department, the restructuring of Departments into Aireacht/Executive Units, the application of cost-effectiveness techniques to public service programmes, and the planned development of public service staff.

7. Advisory Bodies

A democratic government needs wide backing for its policies if it is to be successful. The people, however, can be directly consulted only on rare occasions. Governments, then, seeking a broad consensus and realising the value of prior consultation with key groups, often resort to advisory bodies composed of experts from outside the public service and representatives of organisations and groups with an interest in the particular matter that calls for policy decision.

Commissions of inquiry

Commissions of inquiry are established to advise the government on some broad national problem. The appropriate minister usually issues a warrant of appointment, naming the members of the commission and giving their terms of reference. The number on a commission varies — there may be as few as eight or as many as twenty-eight. The chairman of the commission is frequently a judge. The other members may be experts, civil servants, or laymen with an interest in the matter under investigation. Service on a commission of inquiry is part-time. The secretary of the commission is a civil servant.

A commission will gather all necessary information and take evidence, both written and oral, from the public. Following its discussions on the information and evidence, the commission will reach agreement on the recommendations it will make to the government. Its report (which may well be several hundred pages in length) embodies the commission's findings as regards facts and also its conclusions. If some members of the commission disagree with the final draft of the report, they may submit a minority report.

The government, having considered the report, may decide

to publish it, thus creating public discussion and debate. If there is strong public support for the recommendations of the commission, the government find themselves in a favourable position politically to implement policy based on the report.

Expert committees

These committees are composed largely of experts from outside the central government departments, together with a few officials from the interested department. Their task is to make a critical examination of a particular problem and submit a report on it to the minister of the department that established the committee. An example of such a committee is the Food Advisory Committee (Department of Health). Members of an expert committee are often drawn from interested groups though not primarily as representatives of such groups. A committee of experts is usually allowed to proceed independently on its own course without much influence being brought to bear by the sponsoring department, although it can be expected that the views of the department are made known to the committee by the official members.

Consultative committees

Consultative committees are established to give government officials an opportunity, in an official way, to discuss matters of mutual interest with people from outside the government service. They are composed of representatives of interest groups asked by the establishing minister to nominate members. Ministers can consult these committees to elicit their reactions to proposed policy moves in their area of interest and receive recommendations from them.

Advisory bodies which in fact administer

There is a number of committees which, though advisory in form, in fact administer some programme. An example is the National Savings Committee (Department of Finance) whose job is to encourage people to save money.

Inter-departmental committees

These are committees composed of civil servants from two or more departments interested in a specialised problem such as foreign trade or civil defence. There are many reasons why the government or a department may establish an inter-departmental rather than an 'outside' committee. In some cases only an inter-departmental committee can adequately do the job as, for example, when the problem concerns the every-day work of departments. In other cases matters of state or national security are involved and secrecy is secured by appointing an inter-departmental committee. Again the government may consider a problem too 'hot' a political issue to assign to an outside agency.

Inter-departmental committees sometimes take evidence from outside persons and organisations and, of course, then their existence becomes publicly known. Sometimes, too, their existence is revealed in the Dáil when a minister, pressed on some problem, says 'there is an inter-departmental committee working on it and we are awaiting its report'.

The reports of inter-departmental committees are nearly always considered to be the private advice of civil servants to their ministers but from time to time reports that bear on matters of considerable public interest are published.

Interest groups

Some of the large interest groups that nominate representatives to serve on advisory bodies are: the Irish Farmers' Association, the Federated Union of Employers, the Irish Congress of Trade Unions, the Irish National Teachers' Organisation, the Confederation of Irish Industry. Such groups are, in general, favourable to the use of advisory committees. In fact they often suggest the establishment of an advisory committee to study problems which they consider important. But some problems do arise for them: sometimes they have not enough senior staff to serve on all the committees they are interested in, sometimes they are not given representation when they feel they should have been, sometimes they are faced with the question of to what extent their organisation is committed to upholding a report signed by their representative.

8. State Finances

As well as the traditional duties of preserving law and order and protecting the country from aggression, modern governments have assumed two other important functions: they take measures to increase the country's wealth and accept responsibility for improving the welfare of the poor. Through taxation they channel money from the better-off sections of the community to the weaker sections either directly e.g. through old age pensions and children's allowances or indirectly by providing free services e.g. health services.

To increase the country's wealth, money must be spent on projects which will produce goods and services. The community, then, must save for this purpose by putting money in banks, in the Post Office Savings Bank, by buying Prize Bonds or investing in Exchequer Bills or in National Loans. The government encourages saving in various ways but particularly by the general promotional work of the National Savings Committee.

Since Ireland cannot produce all the goods it needs to raise its standard of living, it has to import. To pay for imports it has to export to other countries. The government must keep an eye on the balance of trade. If the value of imports exceeds that of exports over a long period, then corrective measures must be taken to balance imports and exports. Ideally an expansion of exports is the solution but this cannot always be achieved quickly and if the deficit in our payments is serious, reduction of imports may be necessary, leading very probably to reductions in employment and consequently in the average living standard.

For many years now Ireland has had a substantial adverse trade balance — in 1976 it was £450 million — and yet the country is able to sustain it. How so? The fact is that we pay for imports by our exports of goods plus other money earned abroad or from foreigners. A big source of this other money is transportation. In 1976, the latest year for which detailed figures are available, Ireland earned £125 million from abroad on freight and passenger services and spent only £40 million abroad itself. That put £85 million against the adverse trade balance. Tourism is another contributor. Foreign tourists and travellers spent £137 million in Ireland in 1976 while Irish people touring or travelling abroad spent £109 million. That put a further £28 million against the adverse trade balance. Income from capital is another factor. In 1976 income from investments made by Irish people in foreign enterprises came to £169 million, while income from investments made by foreigners in Ireland came to £184 million, thus making a disimprovement under this heading of £15 million. Ireland receives grants from various EEC funds. In 1976 these amounted to £146 million. Ireland also contributes to the EEC budget. In 1976 we contributed £54 million. Thus we gained £92 million to set against the adverse trade balance. Emigrants' remittances, pensions and allowances because of service in foreign forces or commercial firms and money left in wills formed a group that brought in £93 million and sent out only £10 million. Thus another £83 million was gained to set against the adverse trade balance. Finally, from other services such as the foreign commission earned by import agents and the provision of diplomatic and military services abroad the balance in Ireland's favour was £30 million. In 1976, then, there was £303 million from all these sources to set against the £450 million adverse trade balance: our

TABLE 1: Non-Trade Income

	Contribution (£ millions) in 1976
Freight and passenger services	+ 85
Tourism	+ 28
Income from capital	− 15
EEC transactions	+ 92
Emigrants' remittances, pensions etc.	+ 83
Foreign commission etc.	+ 30
TOTAL	+ 303

overspending was reduced to £147 million. This, however, was covered by the net inflow of foreign capital into Ireland in that year. Most of this resulted from the attraction of money from abroad by the banking system and by business investment opportunities. The rest of it, however, resulted from borrowings from abroad by the government. Such borrowing, of course, could not be sustained over an indefinite period.

State spending

The provision of state services involves large expenditure by the government itself. Social services such as old age pensions, unemployment assistance and unemployment insurance and health services account for a great deal of the expenditure. Education (construction of schools and universities, grants to schools and universities, salaries of teachers), advisory services, financial assistance to industry and agriculture, defence and law enforcement and the salaries of civil servants use up most of the rest. The cost of these services changes from year to year. As we have seen the government present the Estimates for Public Services to the Dáil in December. The estimates for 1978 were £2,119 million. Expenditure on health, education and social welfare accounted for almost half of this total.

TABLE 2: 1978 estimates for Health, Education and Social Welfare

	Estimate (£ million)	Per Cent
Health	357	17.0
Education	349	16.5
Social Welfare	309	14.6
Totals	1,015	48.0
Total estimates for Public Services	2,119	100.0

A large part of government expenditure relates to capital projects — land improvement, afforestation, aid to hotels and tourist resorts, shipping, aviation, loans to private housing through the local authorities, grants or repayable loans to some state-sponsored bodies, improvement of telephone communication. Part of the cost of these services is included in the annual Book of Estimates under the heading of Voted Capital Services. The estimates for voted capital services for 1978 amounted to £250 million out of the £2,119 million total. Provision for other capital expenditure is made in the capital budget, a document presented to the Dáil in conjunction with the annual budget for current services. The provision for this other expenditure in the capital budget for 1978 was £516 million, so that the total capital expenditure for the year was estimated at £766 million. (Part of the capital budget each year provides for the repayment of debts created by state borrowing.) Adding the current and capital expenditures together, the total estimate for 1978 came to £2,635 million. Where does the state get this money from?

State revenue

The money the state needs it gets mainly from taxes: it also has a number of non-tax sources of revenue; and if it needs more money to cover expenditure it borrows from financial institutions at home and abroad.

Income tax is the biggest source of tax revenue. It is a direct tax on income arising within the state and is, therefore, payable even by persons resident outside the state who derive income within the state. In 1978 income tax was expected to yield £664 million. *Excise duties* are taxes on certain goods produced or activities carried on within the state — tax on cigarettes, beer, spirits, oils, betting, for example. In 1978 excise duties were expected to yield £477 million. *Value added tax* (VAT) is a general sales tax applied, at all stages of production and distribution, to sales of goods and rendering of services. In 1978 VAT was expected to yield £386 million. *Corporation profits tax* is a tax on the profits of limited liability companies. In 1978 it was expected to yield £108 million. *Stamp duties* (payments for stamps that must be impressed on certain documents such as cheques, deeds, insurances), *customs duties* (levies on goods from outside the EEC in line with the Community common tariff), *motor vehicle duties* (levied on private motor cars and commercial vehicles over a certain horse-power), *capital taxes* (taxes on certain transfers of wealth), *agricultural levies* (taxes on agricultural goods or inputs imported from countries outside the EEC) make up the remaining sources of revenue. In 1978 these were expected to yield £105 million.

TABLE 3: Tax Revenue 1978 (estimated)

	£ million
Income tax	664
Excise duties	477
Value added tax	386
Corporation profits tax	108
Stamp duties etc	105
TOTAL	1,740

Non-tax revenue comes mainly from the Post Office (postal, telephone and telegraph services), land annuities (repayments by farmers on loans to buy out their land), interest on money loaned to state-sponsored bodies such as Bord na Móna and the ESB, broadcasting licences and profits made by the Central Bank. In 1978 non-tax revenue was expected to come to £310 million.

Tax and non-tax revenue, therefore, was expected to amount to £2,050 million. However, since current and capital expenditure for the year was expected to come to £2,635 million the government expected to borrow £585 million. To complete our general picture of the government's finances we need to advert to one other substantial element — the servicing of the national debt: in 1978 the government expected that it would need £450 million to pay the interest on previous borrowings. A large part of this is met by repayments from local authorities and state-sponsored bodies on advances made to them. In 1978 their contribution was expected to come to £214 million, leaving £236 million to be added to the government's borrowing requirement of £585 million.

The state borrows from banks, insurance companies, and the general public (through national loans, Exchequer Bills, prize bonds, post office savings) and also from financial institutions abroad. How does it pay this money back? Some capital projects pay for themselves — housing loans, some loans to state-sponsored bodies. Others have to be added to the National Debt and paid for out of taxation. It is necessary, then, that a proportion of the government's capital projects should at least indirectly help to increase the wealth of the country because then government revenue can be increased without increasing the already high rate of taxation.

The Central Bank

In Ireland the Central Bank, which was set up by the state in 1943, has important responsibilities in regard to the money supply in the country. The Central Bank is the authority that issues Irish currency. At present there is about £403 million of Irish legal tender notes in circulation and about £26 million in coins. The Central Bank holds the gold, sterling, dollars and the securities which give backing to the Irish issue. (British coin also circulates freely in Ireland and during the tourist season American dollars are to be found in many a shop-keeper's till.)

In addition, the Central Bank has powers to regulate to a large extent the amount which the commercial banks in the country lend to borrowers. Governments have to have some control over credit. If a good proportion of the borrowed money is not used productively, then the effect of bank credit is to increase the supply of money to a greater extent than the volume of goods. This can lead to inflation which involves a rise in prices and an increase of imports relative to exports with consequent deterioration in the balance of payments.

9. Local Government

Virtually every country has, in addition to central agencies with nationwide concerns, a system of local administration carried on by a variety of local bodies with locally limited jurisdiction. Such bodies generally serve a double purpose: they administer a number of important services (roads, housing, health, education are notable examples) in their areas, and, secondly, they furnish a means by which local communities and the people who form part of them can fairly readily participate in the process of government and administration. They are thus in a sense schools of democracy, as well as organs of state action, in the wider meaning of the term.

There are many kinds of local bodies. They vary in size, composition and function from the largest regional health board which may serve more than a million inhabitants to the small town commissions providing a very limited range of services (housing, public lighting perhaps, a town hall) for a population of a few thousand. The membership of a local body may be either directly elected, as a county council is, or nominated in whole or in part by an elected body, like a county committee of agriculture. Local bodies are also financed, to a varying degree, from local taxation, or rates. And they enjoy a certain degree of local autonomy in making decisions or working out local policies.

Another point worth mentioning about local bodies is that their discretion and ability to act is clearly circumscribed by law. The state has delegated a wide range of different powers to them, and closely supervises their operations. The Public Services Organisation Review Group (the Devlin Committee, which reported in 1969) regarded local bodies as in large measure appendages of government departments or, as they expressed it, executive agencies of the departments. Thus the major role of county and city councils, borough councils and urban district councils is to carry out the policies and aims of the Department of the Environment in matters such as housing, roads and traffic, and environmental services. The Department of Health, in pursuance of the national aim of better health services, works through regional health boards. The Department of Education organises vocational education through local vocational education committees and the Department of Agriculture provides advisory services with the help of county committees of agriculture. Various other departments operate through local bodies for certain services: the Department of Defence in relation to civil defence is a good example.

County and other councils

The term 'local government' is applied, strictly speaking, to the activities of a group of directly elected authorities — county councils, county borough councils, and a number of smaller urban bodies which conduct their business under the general supervision of the Department of the Environment.

For the purpose of local government, the Republic of Ireland is divided into 31 major units known as administrative counties. For the 27 rural administrative counties — there are 27 because Tipperary County is divided into two administrative counties known as the North Riding and the South Riding — a county council is elected and for the four largest cities, Dublin, Cork, Limerick and Waterford, which rank as administrative counties, a county borough council is elected. A great deal of the work necessary for the benefit of the people in these areas has been assigned to the councils.

County councils vary in membership from 21 to 31, except Cork which has 46 members. Dublin County Borough Council has 45 members, Cork 31, Limerick 17 and Waterford 15. A county council consists of a chairman and councillors, a county borough council consists of a mayor (in Dublin and Cork called the Lord Mayor) aldermen and councillors. The aldermen are the candidates in each electoral area who get the highest votes at elections. Dublin has 9 aldermen, Cork 6, Limerick and Waterford 5.

Councils of counties and county boroughs are elected by the local government electors for a term of five years. The local government electors are the persons whose names are on the register of electors. The register comes into force on 15 April of each year. Any person who is eighteen years of age or over on that date is entitled to be registered in the area in which he was ordinarily resident on the previous 15 September. Elections are held under the proportional representation system. For convenience, the counties and county boroughs are divided into electoral areas.

The candidate may be nominated by himself or by a local government elector for the area concerned. When the elections are due, public notices are issued in each area indicating where forms are to be obtained and giving details of the latest dates for considering nominations. Unlike members of the Oireachtas, councillors are not paid for their services. Some allowances, however, are made to meet their subsistence and travelling expenses.

County council meetings

If the candidate is successful in the election, the county secretary sends him notice of the annual meeting which is held fourteen days after the election. The first business at this meeting is the election of the chairman and vice-chairman. The council then proceeds to select members for its various committees and for those bodies on which it has representatives. The following are some of the more important ones — the county committee of agriculture, the county vocational education committee, the regional health board and regional development organisation.

Where there are joint committees, the council selects members to represent it, e.g. on a joint library committee, or joint drainage committee. It can be seen therefore that a member has a chance of selecting membership of some committee in which he has a special interest. Much will depend on the amount of time he feels he can devote to the work.

Generally speaking, county council meetings are open to the public and press representatives attend. Many of the statutory committees, i.e. committees which by law must be set up, such as the agriculture and vocational education committees, meet in public with press representatives in attendance. All authorities, however, have the right to go into committee and discuss special issues in private. The decisions arrived at are then subject to confirmation at an ordinary council meeting.

Each member receives an agenda at least three days before the meeting, setting out the work proposed to be done at that meeting. A member can also send in a notice that he proposes to raise some matter at a meeting and this will be placed on the agenda under the heading 'Notice of Motion'.

Procedure at meetings is governed by the standing orders of the council, which are the usual rules required for the orderly conduct of meetings. Decisions are taken usually by the majority of members present who vote on an issue. For every authority a quorum is fixed of one fourth the total membership and business cannot start unless that number of members is present. Minutes of each meeting are kept and copies circulated to each member with the agenda for the next meeting. The first business at each ordinary meeting is to confirm the minutes of the previous meeting and when the chairman has signed the minutes they cannot be questioned as a record. The county secretary is responsible for the preparation of the minutes and for ensuring their accuracy. Naturally some of his staff will be present at the meeting to keep track of the details. It is also usual for the county manager to attend all council meetings, and the senior officers, such as county engineer, county secretary and legal adviser, generally attend as well.

Boroughs, urban district councils and town commissions

Boroughs and urban district councils can exercise much the same range of powers as county and city councils. Town commissions are of less significance.

There are seven boroughs, namely Dun Laoghaire, Clonmel, Drogheda, Galway, Kilkenny, Sligo and Wexford, with elected borough councils (fifteen members in Dun Laoghaire and twelve in the others). The council chairman has the title of mayor, except in Dun Laoghaire where he is called Cathaoirleach. The mayor or Cathaoirleach may be paid such yearly expenses as the council may fix.

Urban districts, of which there are 49, resemble boroughs in all respects except that their councils are presided over by chairmen instead of mayors. The urban councils of Bray, Dundalk and Tralee have twelve members, all others nine.

Town commissions (28 in number) have nine-member boards, presided over by chairmen. Unlike the other local authorities described above they cannot strike rates, and their powers and functions are very limited.

A White Paper published by the government in 1971 contained proposals for the abolition of most of the smaller urban authorities, as well as a number of other suggestions for gaining greater efficiency in local government. These plans have not been implemented. A change of government early in 1973 resulted in a new set of proposals involving retention of all local councils but large-scale transfer of powers and functions from urban authorities (apart from city councils) to county councils. A further change of government in 1977 has not produced any new proposals about structure but it is understood that the general re-organisation question is currently under review.

Other local bodies

Regional health boards

The Health Act, 1970, established eight regional authorities, with local advisory committees, to take over the administration of the health services with effect from 1 April 1971. The boards, each of which serves a number of counties, (including county boroughs) are made up of representatives of county and city councils, together with members of the medical, nursing, dental and pharmaceutical professions in the region. Three members of each board are nominated by the Minister for Health. Numbers vary from 27 to 35, a majority in each case being local authority members.

The regional health boards are managed by chief executive officers, and are responsible for all health services, including hospital (in-patient and out-patient) services, general medical services, services for mothers and children, and preventive services. The boards have taken over the operation of all hospitals (mental hospitals as well as general and specialist) formerly under local control. In addition they administer certain welfare services.

To secure rational development of the hospitals system, local and voluntary, the Act of 1970 provides for the establishment of three regional hospital boards based on Dublin, Cork and Galway and covering the whole country. Each is concerned to co-ordinate and develop the hospital services in its area of influence.

A further body, Comhairle na n-Óspidéal carries responsibility at national level for the development of specialist services and staffs in hospitals.

Regional development organisations

Shortly after the Local Government (Planning and Development) Act, 1963, came into effect, it was decided to co-ordinate local development plans on a regional basis. As a further measure of co-ordination, arrangements were made to link environmental and economic development. This was to be done through nine regional development organisations, which are coordinating bodies representing local authorities and other development interests in the various regions, such as the industrial and tourist authorities. Membership includes both elected members and officers of local authorities. Each regional organisation has a director with secretarial staff.

Regional tourism organisations

Eight tourism regions were established by Bord Fáilte in 1964. Each region is serviced by a tourist organisation in the form of a public company, membership of which is open to local authorities, clubs, associations and individuals in the region. The organisations are financed in large part by contributions from Bord Fáilte and local authorities. They engage, in co-operation with Bord Fáilte, in all tourist promotional activities which can be carried out more effectively at regional and local levels. They operate tourist information centres, room reservation services and publicity campaigns, promote entertainment for visitors and exert themselves in many other ways for the benefit of the tourist industry.

Vocational education committees

These are statutory committees of county and county borough councils. Seven borough and urban councils (Bray, Drogheda, Dun Laoghaire, Galway, Sligo, Tralee and Wexford) also have vocational education committees. They provide and manage vocational schools in their areas, and some of them are also concerned with the operation of regional technical colleges.

The committees work under the supervision of the Department of Education which gives substantial subsidies towards the cost of the services. A chief executive officer, working to the committee, carries out the day to day management of the service.

County committees of agriculture

Each county council appoints a special committee to assist in providing advisory and other services relating to agriculture in the county. The committees, now mainly consultative bodies, are financed from local rates and from grants provided by the Department of Agriculture. A county agricultural officer carries out the day to day management of the committee's affairs. The work of giving advice and instruction has been transferred to a new central body known as the National Agricultural Advisory, Education and Research Authority.

County development teams

A number of counties (thirteen in all, mainly in the western part of the country) have set up county development teams. These are small high-level units whose function is to promote economic development by mobilising county resources and stimulating new ideas for development. The teams are made up of the county manager, who acts as chairman, the chairman of the county council, the county agricultural officer, the chief executive officer of the vocational education committee, the regional manager of the Industrial Development Authority and the county engineer. Each team has a secretary who acts as county development officer.

Community councils

Finally, a few words about a form of local body which has come to notice in recent years as affording wider opportunities for participation in local improvements and affairs generally than official local government. The idea is not new. The Local Government Act, 1941, empowered county councils to recognise and delegate functions to councils set up by the inhabitants of a locality for furthering their general social and economic interests. A considerable parish council movement developed during World War II but lost momentum when the emergency passed. The Local Government Act, 1955, gave extended powers of approval to county and county borough councils, but the new impulse was not notably effective.

Community councils or associations have nevertheless begun to spring up in many places. The best-known examples, perhaps, are the Ballyfermot Community Association and the Clondalkin Community Council, both in the Dublin area, but the movement is widespread. Muintir na Tíre is actively engaged in promoting the formation of community bodies in various parts of the country.

Organisation usually takes the form of a confederation of voluntary societies in the area. These bodies nominate members to the central council or committee, but members may also be elected by direct vote of the people. The council of the Ballyfermot Community Association is made up of representatives from five area committees, each of which is built on a system of street committees. The council also includes representatives of educational institutions, business, the Department of Labour, the Eastern Health Board, the credit union and other groups.

Activities are numerous and diverse but there are a number of standard functions such as surveying the needs of the community for services and facilities. Councils may also undertake projects such as sports fields, community centres and swimming pools. They may bring community opinion to bear on official bodies whose operations affect their areas. Community councils may act in these and many other ways to give the people a sense of participation in local affairs and in decisions affecting the life of their community.

Work of local authorities

County, city, borough and urban councils have a broad range of interrelated functions — physical planning, roads and road traffic, housing, water supply, sewerage and drainage, coast protection, the fire service etc. — whose common purpose is to achieve a better environment for healthy living and for economic and social development. These councils have, in addition, a number of educational, cultural and welfare functions which are described briefly below.

Planning and development

These are now the most significant functions of county (as well as city and urban district) councils, and carry the greatest potential for beneficial change and development in the environment surrounding our lives. The Local Government (Planning and Development) Act, 1963, which came into operation on 1 October 1964 introduced a comprehensive and flexible system of planning designed to secure orderly development, the preservation of amenities in both urban and rural areas, and the adoption of effective programmes in such matters as urbanisation, traffic, road safety, urban renewal and the environment. The prime instrument in the planning armoury is the development plan which each planning authority must draw up for a five-year period. It sets out development objectives, and is in the form of a written statement, supplemented by maps and plans.

The objectives must include, in cities and towns:
— land zoning for residential, industrial and other uses
— traffic needs, present and future, including the needs of pedestrians
— development and renewal of obsolete areas
— preserving, improving and extending amenities.

Plans for rural areas must cater for the two last mentioned together with
— new and extended water supplies and sewerage services.

Development plans may, of course, specify other objectives such as conservation of sites, areas or features of natural beauty or special scientific value, buildings of artistic or historic interest; protection of trees and woodlands, and preservation of public rights of way.

Permission from the planning authority must be sought for most kinds of development, such as building, excavation, demolition, extension and other works in or on land and making any material change in the use of structures or land. An applicant may, within a period appeal against the planning authority's decision to a new planning board established under the Local Government (Planning and Development) Act, 1976.

In addition to their control and regulatory functions, planning authorities may exercise a considerable range of positive powers for the benefit of their areas — acquiring and developing land, especially for urban renewal; providing industrial estates and factory sites, and many other facilities for commercial and community benefit.

Roads

The county council is responsible for the maintenance of roads in its area and for main roads in urban district areas. Modern methods of road improvement and maintenance require large investment by the county councils in machinery such as road rollers, tankers for bulk tar distribution, lorries for stone and gravel distribution, quarry machinery such as crushers, excavators, loaders, compressors and mechanical shovels.

In most areas, central stores and machinery yards for maintenance and repairs have been set up. Many skilled men such as fitters and mechanics are now employed.

Because of the rapid growth in road traffic in recent times a need for the improvement of the major inter-urban roads has arisen. To cope with the most critical stretches, the Local Government (Roads and Motorways) Act, 1974, empowers local authorities to construct motorways — limited access highways confined to certain types of traffic — and provide modern facilities such as dual carriageways, central medians, flyovers, traffic route lighting, and the like. A system of national primary and national secondary roads has been worked out on the basis of studies carried out by An Foras Forbartha (the National Institute for Physical Planning and Construction Research). Under the 1974 Act reinforced powers of direction and control in the planning, improvement and construction of national roads are available to the Minister for the Environment. Over 3,200 miles of major roads have been designated as national roads.

In general, the law on the construction and maintenance of roads applies to bridges. Where, however, a bridge is to span a river separating two administrative areas, or will be of particular service to a number of areas, the question of who should build, pay for and maintain it, arises. The Minister for the

Environment may make a bridge order setting out the authority to build and maintain the bridge, the authorities to pay for it and their respective contributions. Such an order will also determine the site of the bridge and whether or not it is to have an opening span, matters frequently the subject of contention.

The Minister for the Environment has a number of very important functions in relation to road traffic and safety. These include the organisation, through his department, of a network of driver testing centres for the screening of applicants for full driving licences; and the conduct, through the National Road Safety Association, of a programme of road safety measures. The Association also operates a voluntary vehicle inspection service.

Following the passage through the Oireachtas of the Road Traffic (Amendment) Act, 1978, the campaign against drunken drivers, which had run into major legal obstacles, was energetically resumed.

Housing

The eradication of unfit housing, and the replacement of unhealthy, overcrowded dwellings by new houses and flats with adequate space, facilities and equipment are among the most important functions of local authorities. County and city councils have large programmes on hand of site acquisitions and development, and housebuilding. It is their duty to survey the housing situation in their areas from time to time and to assess the needs of their inhabitants for new accommodation. They must take steps to provide houses or flats for those unable to house themselves and their families. They can also assist others by means of loans and grants to build or reconstruct houses for themselves or for sale or letting.

Special arrangements have been made by which local authorities, in co-operation with the National Building Agency, may assist in the housing of key industrial workers brought into an area for new or expanding plants. The National Building Agency may also engage in the provision of houses for local authorities on an agency basis.

Water supply and sewerage

A major function of county and city councils and other urban authorities is the execution of programmes of public water supplies and drainage. These gain importance both from the growth of urban and rural housing, and from the pressures of industrialisation creating demands for water and for methods of disposal of industrial wastes. Tourism and, to an increasing extent, agriculture add their quota to the expanding needs for these facilities.

Environmental protection

Under this heading local authorities operate a complex of services whose general aim is the conservation and enhancement of the environment. They include waste collection and disposal, the provision and maintenance of burial grounds and measures to ensure the safety of structures and places.

The Local Government (Water Pollution) Act, 1977, provides an updated statutory framework for preserving and improving the quality of water in lakes, rivers and estuaries. Local authorities are also empowered to control or prevent atmospheric pollution.

The Irish Water Safety Association is active in promoting water safety by means of instruction courses in swimming, lifesaving and resuscitation. Local authorities co-operate in this work by contributing towards the Association's expenses, employing life-guards at beaches and so on.

The fire service, a local service of great importance, has developed rapidly in recent years. All local authorities, except town commissioners, are fire brigade authorities, but in practice the fire service is provided almost wholly by county councils and county borough corporations. The service has two main aspects: (1) operation of fire brigades, and (2) fire prevention, including the provision of safeguards and means of escape. Local authorities also play a prominent part in civil defence planning, staffing and in the recruitment of volunteers.

Recreation and amenity

Local authorities have a wide range of powers enabling them to equip their areas with recreation facilities. They may construct swimming pools or help private groups to take on the job. The Local Government (Sanitary Services) Act, 1948, and earlier Acts contain provisions for parks, open spaces, playing fields and sports facilities. The Local Government Act, 1941, enables county councils to provide parish halls or offices for approved local councils, and the Local Government Act, 1955, empowers local authorities to give grants towards the building of such halls.

The library service is local government's main cultural activity. Libraries are built, stocked, staffed and maintained by city and county councils, as well as by a few other urban authorities. Advice and assistance in planning and running the service are available from An Chomhairle Leabharlanna (the Library Council), a central body whose members are appointed by the Minister for the Environment.

A growing number of local authorities have provided civic museums and art galleries. Urban authorities may provide theatres or subsidise the building of opera houses.

The Local Government (Planning and Development) Act, 1963, requires planning authorities to preserve and develop local amenities. The Department of the Environment operates an important scheme of grants designed to assist local authorities and local voluntary bodies (community councils, local development associations and others) to improve amenities in their areas.

In 1977 the Minister for the Environment introduced, as part of the Government's job creation programme, a scheme of grants to local authorities for works of an environmental character. The amounts allocated to each area were related to local unemployment figures.

Itinerants (travelling people)

Local authorities are the principal agencies for the furtherance of the government's attempt to improve the living conditions of itinerants and facilitate their absorption into the community. Where travelling people opt to settle, local authorities can provide housing. For families who have no interest at present in permanent settlement, camping-sites are provided. These sites serve also the needs of families who require a period of adjustment before finally quitting their wandering way of life.

Other services

These include a wide variety of works, grants and facilities, some connected with the predominantly environmental role of local government, others a survival from times when the functions of local authorities were more comprehensive in scope. They range from university grants and scholarships to the provision of pounds for stray animals, the construction and maintenance of courthouses, piers and harbours, schemes for credit financing of fertiliser and seed purchase, the preparation of voters' and jurors' lists, the provision of school meals, and the administration of weights and measures, gas supplies, abattoirs and a dwindling number of fairs and markets.

County and city management

The Irish system of local government (i.e. county and city councils, borough and urban district councils and boards of town commissioners) is characterised by a unique organisational pattern. In brief the work of every local authority is divided into two categories: (1) major or policy functions, performed by the elected members in council, and (2) executive functions, performed by the county or city manager as the case may be.

City management is an American idea. It evolved about the beginning of this century from the reform movement in United States cities and was picked up and remodelled to suit conditions in Ireland in the 1920s. The system was first applied in Cork by the Cork City Management Act, 1929, then in Dublin and Dun Laoghaire in 1930; Limerick followed in 1934 and Waterford in 1939. After a short interval, county management was introduced in 1942, and as the county manager became also manager for each borough, urban district or town in his area, this meant that from 1942 onwards the management system applied uniformly throughout the country.

Provision was made for certain joint arrangements. In Dublin, the city manager acts also as county manager for the county, including Dun Laoghaire borough. With the aid of a number of assistant city and county managers he copes with the formidable problems — in planning, roads, streets etc. — of the rapidly growing Dublin complex. Certain managers still act for two counties — Laois and Offaly, and Westmeath-

Longford — but the trend has been towards separate single county managers. A recent effort to link Cork city and county under a single manager proved abortive.

The functions of local authorities are of two kinds: reserved and executive. Reserved powers are exerciseable only by the elected bodies, and include budgeting, taxation and borrowing; making bye-laws; adopting development plans, and a number of other policy matters. Executive functions are performed by managers and comprise the appointment, control and discipline of staff, and the multitude of decisions which go to make up the day-to-day business of local authorities.

The council control of finance is exercised in the following ways: (1) the manager must prepare an estimate each year showing the amounts required for each service, (2) the estimate is examined by the council and a final amount adopted by them, (3) this forms the basis for the rate for the coming year and the manager cannot exceed the figures allowed without the council's permission, (4) the manager cannot add any members to the permanent staff of the council unless the council agrees, (5) the manager cannot increase or decrease the remuneration of the staff without the council's approval, (6) the council must approve of any proposal to borrow money for the work of the council.

The elected members of the council can exercise certain control over the executive functions. The members may by resolution direct the manager to inform them before he performs any executive function which they specify. They may direct him not to proceed with any particular work. They may also, by resolution passed after due notice, require the manager to do anything within his executive powers. These powers of the council do not apply to staff matters.

It must not be inferred from these legal definitions that the council and the manager are in constant opposition on these matters. At council and committee meetings there are many opportunities for the elected members to discuss informally with the manager matters that may come strictly within the executive functions. Again, at estimates time and during the year, the elected members are glad to get the views of the manager on policy questions which they themselves have to decide. The actual working of the management system is generally harmonious. Councils and managers co-operate to do their best for the people they serve.

Staff of local bodies

The increasing responsibilities of local administration have called for improved standards of efficiency in the ordinary day-to-day work. Recruitment to the general clerical staff is by way of competitive examination and a certain number of higher posts may be filled by promotion from that grade. The more senior posts are generally filled through the Local Appointments Commission. Vacancies for managers and assistant managers, chief executive officers, county secretaries, county accountants, town clerks, city accountants and some other senior posts are filled by persons selected, after interview, by the Local Appointments Commission. Engineering, medical, and other professional posts are also filled through the Local Appointments Commission.

Finances

How much does this activity cost? Naturally, the variety and extent of local activities (aggregate numbers employed amount to about 63,000, including the staffs of health boards) add up to a sizeable annual expenditure. This is currently (1978) running at the rate per annum of over £770 million on revenue account and over £166 million for capital projects. The figure for running costs represents outlay by county and city councils, boroughs, urban districts and towns, in addition to regional health boards, vocational education committees and committees of agriculture. Nearly 90 per cent of capital expenditure goes on housing, water and sewerage etc., the next biggest item being vocational schools, with hospitals, harbours and courthouses making up the remainder.

Where does the money come from? Over the last few years the proportion supplied by rate-payers has fallen dramatically, and of the £770 million used for day-to-day expenses less than one tenth now comes from rates, with close on £630 million contributed from the Exchequer. The balance is made up of house rents together with miscellaneous fees of various kinds. The State contribution of £630 million comes to local bodies in the form of substantial grants towards the cost of health services, housing, roads, water and sewerage schemes and a list of other items. Major constituents are two substantial grants in relief of rates: one over £80 million for the de-rating of domestic premises (homes, flats, secondary schools and community halls); and the agricultural grant (now £38.5 million a year) paid in relief of rates on agricultural land.

In recent years the state has assumed liability for virtually the whole of the cost of two important services, part of which were local charges. These are local authority housing schemes, and health services. The Road Fund whose income was derived mainly from motor taxation was abolished in 1978 following the decision to abolish taxes on most private motor cars. Road grants formerly paid from the Fund are now met by the Exchequer.

Rates are a local tax on real property — mainly buildings and lands. Dwellings have been de-rated but are still rateable, with the significant change that domestic rates are now paid by the state, not by the occupiers. Shops, offices, hotels, factories and business premises generally continue to be liable to rates. The mechanism of assessment involves determination of the annual value or 'valuation' of each parcel of property by a state officer called the Commissioner of Valuation, who hands a list of such valuations to each rating authority before the commencement of every financial year. The rating authorities, comprising county and city councils, borough and urban district councils, then fix or strike a rate in the pound sufficient to bring in their estimated net requirements for the year ahead, taking account of (1) the current valuation list and (2) income from all other sources such as state grants, rents, fees etc. Rates are in general paid by the occupiers of property.

Town commissioners are not now rating authorities, but may demand what they require to meet their expenses from the county council for the area. The amount supplied by the county council is then assessed on properties in the town by way of special town charge.

The local financial year has been, since 1975, co-terminous with the calendar year.

Money required for capital purposes is almost invariably borrowed from a state source called the Local Loans Fund, managed by the Commissioners of Public Works. Repayment may be spread over varying periods up to a maximum of fifty years. Capital for hospitals and other health services is supplied in large part by the Hospitals Trust Fund, which is fed by the proceeds of four sweepstakes organised and run each year by Hospitals Trust (1940) Ltd.

General

Local government and other forms of local administration give local people a say in the provision of many important public services in their area. The county and other councils, regional boards and committees, are in many ways like small parliaments and indeed it is common practice for the fledgling politician who aspires to the national parliament to gain experience in the art of politics and extend his influence among the people by serving as a local representative in a county council or other local body.

The local councillor represents the people's interest in the formulation of policy and the spending of money. More important, perhaps, he explains policy to the people. He makes representations on behalf of the individual whose particular case is not sympathetically treated by the operation of general regulations.

Local government creates many of the conditions necessary for civilised living. Like some of the state-sponsored bodies it helps to bring about that physical development of our country that the setting up of new industries demands. A local council can be viewed as the local community in action. While central government departments exercise a large measure of control over it (mainly through the government grants) the quality and amount of the activity of a local body largely influences and reflects the prosperity, enterprise and civic pride of the local community.

10. State-Sponsored Bodies

The value of money is directly related to the number of things we can exchange it for; and ever since the Industrial Revolution, the introduction of mass production methods by Henry Ford and the modern break-through in the application of science, the number of things that money can buy has progressively multiplied. Standards of living have shot up.

A country that has few manufacturing industries must import to raise its living standards. To pay for imports it has, broadly speaking, to export the goods it does produce — agricultural goods. Unfortunately, there is normally (in peacetime) a surplus of agricultural goods on the world market and so prices are low. The amount of goods a mainly agricultural country can afford to import is therefore small: its standards of living remain low.

In 1922 prospects for the Irish Free State were bleak. There were few industries in the country, educational standards were low, roads were bad, housing worse and such social services as existed were degrading to a proud people. Moreover, there was the problem of emigration: people left the country to seek higher living standards in Britain and America. The introduction of machinery to the farms reduced the number of jobs at home and swelled the number of emigrants. Emigration from the countryside hit the villages and small towns whose trade depended on the rural population round about them; that, together with the lack of industrial investment is why emigration from villages and towns became a later trend in Irish emigration. However, agriculture was experiencing a boom owing to post-war scarcity and it was agricultural export earnings that sustained the state in its cradle years.

A solution to Ireland's economic problems was to set up

industries — but this in itself posed gigantic problems. An industry needs, first of all, capital — money for buildings and plant: a new turbulent state does not attract the private investor. Raw materials should be readily available: such resources were scarce in Ireland. There must be abundant and cheap supplies of power: Ireland had no significant coal or gas deposits, no oil, no hydro-electric scheme. Industry requires a well-developed infra-structure; for instance, there must be good land, sea and air services so that manufactured goods can be transported quickly and cheaply to marketing centres; there must be good telephonic, telegraphic and postal systems so that orders can be handled efficiently; there must be good schools, colleges and universities capable of turning out the kind of people needed by industry and commerce — skilled workers of all kinds, managers, designers, architects, accountants, engineers; there must be hospitals, houses, libraries, cinemas, radio, dance halls and all those services which people require for normal contented living: compared with other western countries at the time, the Irish infrastructure was grossly under-developed.

Such was the internal situation. External conditions were equally grim. Inflation followed in the wake of World War I, with too much money chasing too few goods. This meant that imports of industrial goods were dear and — what was worse for a country that might hope to build up its own industry — the machinery needed to manufacture consumer goods was also scarce. Moreover, there were no international agencies such as exist today with the funds to aid newly-emergent states.

For thirty-five years the state turned inwardly upon itself, shutting out an inhospitable world. Successive governments promoted agriculture, encouraged and protected native light industry — such as cloth manufacture and leather work — with massive tariffs, and built up the country's infrastructure. This last task involved enormous social investment, i.e. capital had to be invested in work which, while it raised living standards, did not bring in a return which could be re-invested. In all this work, the departments of state were active, e.g. the Department of the Environment looked after the provision of housing, roads, hospitals and water supplies, the Department of Education looked after the provision of new national schools, and the subsidisation of colleges and universities. But in bringing the country to its present state of development where it can carry modern industry, a major role was played by a number of organisations called state-sponsored bodies.

Everyone in Ireland has a rough idea of what is meant by the phrase 'state-sponsored bodies' — organisations like Aer Lingus, Córas Iompair Éireann, the Electricity Supply Board, Bord na Móna. However, it is difficult to define them exactly. They are not part of the civil service yet they belong to the public sector of the economy, not the private enterprise sector. They have been defined as permanent, autonomous public bodies whose staff is not drawn from the civil service, but to whose board or council the government or ministers in the government appoint directors or council members.

State-sponsored bodies are, from the point of view of their establishment, of two main types. They may be established by a minister in the form of a public or private company; or by an Act of the Oireachtas which specifies the constitution of the body, the amount of public money to be invested in it, and the minister responsible for appointing the board members nominated by the state. These latter kind are known as statutory corporations. From the point of view of their financial objectives, state-sponsored bodies may be divided, as they were in the Devlin Report on public service organisation, into commercial and non-commercial bodies.

There are over eighty state-sponsored bodies fulfilling a great variety of functions. There follows an outline of some of the most familiar.

Power

Electricity Supply Board (ESB)

Before the state was founded the bulk of our power supply was based on imported fuel. In 1927 the government set up a Board to take charge of electricity supplies. A main objective of the Board was to exploit native resources as much as possible. Two approaches to this end were adopted. On the one hand hydro-electric schemes such as those on the Shannon and the Erne were created, on the other hand the ESB and

Bord na Móna co-operated in the generation of electricity from steam, using peat as the initial source of energy. At present about 35 per cent of the electricity generated is based on peat, water power and native coal. Natural gas from the sea off Kinsale has been brought into use. The ESB is continuing its study of the use of nuclear energy and it has put proposals to the government which aim to diversify the sources of energy used.

The ESB's role in the promotion of the economic and social development of the country is enormous. The use of native resources lowers the volume of imports and creates work at home (the ESB employs about 10,800 people). The Board's industrial rates of charge are kept as low as possible. The Board markets electrical appliances. This not only increases the standards of living of thousands of people but stimulates the demand for electricity. Increased production has meant greater productivity (i.e. lower cost per unit). The social advantages of electricity — one thinks immediately of power for light, home heating, water supply, cinemas, radio, television, theatres and dance halls — were long confined to the towns and cities, but the rural electrification scheme has extended these advantages to the remotest corners of the country: the social life of the country areas has been vastly improved.

Bord na Móna

Bord na Móna was established as a statutory corporation in 1946, replacing the Turf Development Board which dated from 1934. It produces two types of fuel — machine turf and milled peat.

A large part of its output is used by the ESB for electricity generation. The remainder of the machine turf and the milled peat (converted to briquettes) is sold in Ireland. Bord na Móna also produces moss peat for horticultural and other purposes and has established a world-wide market for that product.

People are naturally proud of Bord na Móna. It represents a huge enterprise created by Irishmen out of what were formerly vast tracts of waste-land. Bord na Móna designs and builds its own machinery. It has research stations to investigate means of improving the energy-yield of peat. The bogs consequently yield a clean, convenient and popular fuel.

Transport

We have already seen how industry needs a good transport system. Moreover, commerce is largely dependent on the possibility of moving large quantities of goods from one place to another. The ordinary citizen needs good transport both for business and pleasure.

CIE

In 1945 a state-sponsored body called Córas Iompair Éireann was established to look after public transport by rail and road. For many reasons, public transport all over the world was — and still is — in a sorry condition. First of all, it was in many cases competing with itself — the road services with the rail services, the bus with the train. Secondly, it had to compete with ever-increasing private transport. In Ireland these problems were aggravated by a diminishing rural population.

CIE has mounted a vigorous campaign to improve its services, to give the public a good image of itself and to bring in as much business as possible. It has backed up its efforts by research into business and personal transport needs. It is 'rationalising' its services by cutting out duplication of services and by closing down uneconomic lines. Many people believe that it would be possible for CIE to break even or perhaps to turn a profit if it were not charged by the Oireachtas to maintain uneconomic services because of social needs.

Irish Shipping Ltd

It is a strange fact that Ireland, an island with hundreds of natural harbours and a complex system of rivers and lakes that open up the interior, has not developed until recent years a significant shipping fleet. Irish Shipping Limited came into being during the second world war when foreign vessels were not available to ensure the nation's supply of essential commodities. In 1978, the company's fleet consisted of nine vessels ranging in size from the Irish Elm (39,000 tonnes dead weight) to the jointly owned St. Patrick (5,000 tonnes dead weight). By far the greatest part of the company's business is derived from tramp and charter operations, i.e. from external trade. This means that there is no limit to its possible expansion except that which is set by commercial prudence. It also means that our balance of payments problem is eased by the money earned on foreign freight.

Because of the development of aircraft in modern times, we are inclined to regard the ship as obsolescent. However, at present air-freight accounts for only a minute proportion of world trade and this situation will continue into the foreseeable future. Speed is not always a crucial factor. Ships though slower can transport goods in greater bulk and do it much more cheaply.

B + I

The British and Irish Steampacket Co. Ltd, which became a state-sponsored body in 1965, engages in car, passenger and freight traffic between the Republic and Britain. It is by far the biggest transporter of freight between the Republic and Britain and it is a major transporter of freight between the Republic and the continent. It gives the Irish government, therefore, a major stake in a vital aspect of external trade.

Aer Lingus

Air transport is probably the most competitive business in the world and yet it is a business in which the Irish have been strikingly successful. Aer Lingus started late: its inaugural flight took place on 27 May 1936, when a five-seater de Havilland Dragon took off from Baldonnel (now Casement) Aerodrome, County Dublin for Bristol with five passengers aboard. Today it is a multimillion pound business, carrying over 2 million passengers each year and employing 6,000 people.

Since most people identify Irish civil aviation with Aer Lingus, some confusion arises when reference is made to Aer Rianta and Aerlinte Éireann. Aer Lingus is the company which operates on a network of routes connecting Ireland with Britain and the Continent. Aerlinte Éireann is the company that operates the trans-atlantic routes that link Ireland with New York and Boston. The two companies are legally separate but they are operationally integrated under the common marketing name of Aer Lingus. They have a common management and a joint organisation. Aer Rianta is the Irish airports authority which manages Dublin, Cork and Shannon airports as agents for the Minister for Tourism and Transport.

Aer Lingus is not a large company by international standards. It is, however, one of the most successful national airlines in the world. Like Irish Shipping Ltd it can be treated as an important export industry for most of its operating revenue comes from outside Ireland and most of its expenditure is incurred at home. Its spending on publicity, advertising and promotional campaigns abroad in the interest of tourism exceeds that of any other body. Aer Lingus has also developed a great number of ancillary services which it sells successfully all over the world — hotel and tour operations, computer services, training services and aircraft maintenance. Internally it has been not only a large employer but also one of the great forces at work in the modernisation of Ireland.

Promotion

Bord Fáilte
Tourism is an important source of income to our country. In 1977 our visitors, who numbered almost 2 million, spent £173 million. It is the job of Bord Fáilte to foster this industry. There are two main aspects to Bord Fáilte's work. First, the country itself must be made attractive. The visitor expects good hotel accommodation, good transport facilities, pleasant scenery, places of special interest (such as old castles and abbeys, museums etc.), good beaches, good entertainment, good shops. Much of Bord Fáilte's efforts have been directed towards hotel improvement, the encouragement of tidiness in towns, the development of holiday resorts and angling centres, towards nurturing the souvenir industry, supporting festivals, sign-posting and helping local development committees. Secondly, the country must be 'sold' to the foreign tourist. Bord Fáilte uses all the means of publicity to bring Ireland to the notice of potential tourists. It distributes posters, brochures and informational leaflets among travel agents and transport companies, it publishes its own holiday magazine, *Ireland of the Welcomes*, it issues releases to newspapers and magazines, it invites travel writers and film units to Ireland and of course it engages in straight come-to-Ireland advertising. In order to capture the business convention market it has established the Convention Bureau of Ireland.

In 1964 Bord Fáilte established eight regional tourism organisations, membership of which is open to all persons within the region as well as to local authorities, clubs, associations and other relevant groups. The organisations, which aim to intensify the contribution to tourism of each region, receive financial support from Bord Fáilte and all local authorities.

The foreign money earned by tourism gives considerable ease to our balance of payments problem. Moreover, by presenting a modern image of Ireland the prestige of our exported goods is enhanced. It is clear too that tourism directly increases our standard of living. Tourist revenue subsidises many amenities we ourselves use. Finally tourism helps to raise the general standard of taste throughout the country and the general taste is reflected not only in better houses and tidier towns but in the design of our manufactured goods (good design is a vital factor on the world market). In short, tourism makes Ireland a richer, more beautiful and more interesting country for ourselves and our visitors.

IDA

The Industrial Development Authority, founded in 1949 as an agency of the Department of Industry and Commerce, became an autonomous state-sponsored organisation in April, 1970. At the same time, An Foras Tionscal, the grants board, was dissolved and its functions were transferred to the IDA.

The Authority has national responsibility for the furtherance of industrial development in Ireland. It carries out promotional and publicity programmes at home and abroad; provides grants and other financial facilities for new and existing industry; constructs and administers industrial estates; acquires industrial sites and constructs advance factories or custom-built factories for approved projects at regional locations; promotes joint ventures and licensing agreements; provides financial and advisory services to meet the special needs of small industries; undertakes national and regional industrial planning; evaluates the implications for industrial development in Ireland of EEC proposals and policies. The IDA has established a regional office in each of the nine regions. The Authority has 14 overseas offices which promote Ireland as an industrial location in their territories.

Córas Tráchtála/Irish Export Board

We have already noted the importance of exports. Under heavy tariff protection certain light industries were established in the thirties and forties to serve the home market. The protectionist policy meant that there was little competition for the Irish industrialist and consequently many important commercial aspects were generally neglected — such things as the quality and design of goods, market research, packaging and advertising. When Irish industry expanded further and our industrialists sought export markets they found themselves at a great disadvantage. To help industrialists in their export drive the government set up Córas Tráchtála. Córas Tráchtála engages in market exploration and investigation, provision of marketing information (e.g. on distribution methods, sales procedures, selection of agents, etc.), provision of general information and consultancy service on design, organisation of overseas itineraries for export executives, establishment of liaison between Irish firms and foreign buyers, provision of training facilities at home and abroad for export sales executives, participation in the development of technical assistance projects, co-operation in publicity and in product promotion through overseas offices, exhibitions, trade fairs and retail outlets.

Production

In the thirties, when government policy was directed towards building a self-sufficient state, it was decided that we should produce enough sugar at home to satisfy our needs.

Cómhlucht Siúicre Éireann Teo.

In 1933 Cómhlucht Siúicre Éireann Teo. was established. The new state-sponsored company acquired the existing sugar factory at Carlow and built three more at Mallow, Thurles and Tuam. The early years were very difficult. The economic war with Britain, which was precipitated by the Irish government's refusal to pay further land annuities to Britain, left Irish agriculture severely depressed. The sugar project survived these abnormal conditions and later prospered to such an extent that it was able to satisfy the nation's sugar needs and in addition export a small surplus. The Sugar Company employs about 5,000 people and it has contracts with 22,000 beet-growers.

Erin Foods

Established in 1958 as a subsidiary of the Sugar Company, Erin Foods Ltd processes peas, beans, cabbage, swedes, parsnips, and potatoes. It manufactures soups. External marketing of its products is handled by Heinz, the British-based company. Over 60 per cent of all products manufactured by Erin Foods is sold abroad.

Other Bodies

There are a great number of state-sponsored bodies which, though small in size, carry out extremely important work — in marketing, Córas Beostoic agus Feola Teo. (the Irish Livestock and Meat Board); in finance, the Industrial Credit Company; in health, the Voluntary Health Insurance Board and the Hospitals Trust Board; in communications, Radio Telefís Éireann; in research, the Institute for Industrial Research and Standards and An Foras Talúntais; in production, Ceimici Teoranta and Nitrigin Éireann Teoranta.

General

The state in Ireland employs 260,000 people. Of these, 60,000 are employed by the state-sponsored bodies. CIE with 21,000 and the ESB with 10,800 between them account for more than half of that total. The direct impact of the state-sponsored bodies on the country's economy is clearly very considerable. Their indirect contribution is also important. It is national policy that state organisations should use native materials as much as possible. The ESB, CIE, Bord na Móna and Irish Shipping Ltd are large-scale users of diverse types of equipment and the money they spend has helped to get under way industries which have now developed export trades — the electrical appliance trade is an example, so is ship-building.

Why are state-sponsored bodies established? In answering this question, we must refer to the distinction drawn by the Devlin Committee between two types of state-sponsored body. The first category comprises some twenty 'commercial' organisations which carry on trading activities on behalf of the

state. They produce and sell to the public a variety of commodities or services — electricity (ESB), turf and moss peat
(Bord na Móna), road and passenger services (CIE), air
transport (Aer Lingus) and so on. The reasons for the
establishment of these public enterprises, as they are called,
are many, but they may be summarised as either (1) to fill some
gap left in the economy by private enterprise or (2) to develop
certain native natural resources (sugar beet is a good example)
or (3) to rescue some important undertaking (e.g. Irish Steel
Holdings) which had run into financial difficulties. Where the
task to be undertaken is of a commercial character, most of us
would recognise that the civil service is not geared to take it on.
But there would be little hesitation nowadays in assigning a
new commercial activity, required for government reasons, to
a state-sponsored body operating with the methods and tempo
of private business.

In the second category, comprising some sixty agencies, are
the non-commercial state-sponsored bodies which the Devlin
Committee saw as, each in its different way, carrying out an
executive function of government. Some of these have been
described above — promotional bodies such as Bord Fáilte,
Córas Tráchtála and the Industrial Development Authority;
marketing agencies such as Córas Beostoic agus Feola Teo.;
research bodies like the Institute of Industrial Research and
Standards and An Foras Talúntais, and so on. Now if the
Devlin Committee were correct in regarding the work of these
bodies as an extension of normal state activity, why was it
necessary to create new, semi-independent agencies for these
particular tasks? Why is the work not simply assigned to
government departments? The answer is that the type of
activity concerned seemed to call for a degree of flexibility and
freedom not normally available to civil servants. The work of
the civil service is dominated by two considerations. The first of
these, equity, means that every case handled must get — and
be seen to get — fair treatment; the other, accountability,
means that every action of the civil service whether it involves
money or not can be reviewed by an outside agency — parliament. This is as it should be: it is the basis of public confidence
in the civil service. Civil service procedures then are necessarily
slow. Ordinary commerce is not subject to the same controls

and so it can be carried out with greater freedom and rapidity. The work done by the commercial state-sponsored bodies is ordinary commerce carried out by the state: it needs, therefore, ordinary commercial freedom and so cannot be part of a department.

In the case of non-commercial bodies the argument runs rather differently. The emphasis here lies on the necessity to free ministers from responsibility for the myriad decisions, large and small, which the board and staff of state-sponsored bodies take in the course of day-to-day business. Indeed, as was pointed out in the chapter on the civil service, the Devlin Committee were so impressed by the weight of detail imposed on ministers by the present structure of the civil service, under which they are answerable to parliament for virtually every action taken by civil servants, that they came out in favour of what would in effect be a vast extension of the principle underlying the state-sponsored bodies.

Yet while there is little day-to-day control of state-sponsored bodies, there is very definite control of general policy — which is extremely important. Left to itself a state-sponsored body might well seek the money for expansion from monopolistic profits or loans which, while it might strengthen that organisation, might not, from the point of view of the country as a whole, be put to the best use. For example, at any particular time it might be better to spend money on the encouragement of industry rather than on new jet planes or a new power station. The boards of most state-sponsored bodies are wholly appointed by a minister or ministers. The boards lay down the policies to be followed and see that they are carried out. Naturally the policies of the board must coincide with those of the appropriate minister which means ultimately with the government. Usually the minister keeps personally in touch with the board. The Dáil has the right to debate the policies of state-sponsored bodies and to direct the minister to modify their policies should this appear desirable in the public interest.

There is a general impression that state-sponsored bodies lose money. To clarify the position a distinction must be made. The state-sponsored bodies that are not trading enterprises are dependent on the state for the money needed to provide services. But they cannot fairly be described as 'losing money' or being 'subsidised' by the state any more than a government department 'loses' money or is 'subsidised'. As far as the state trading enterprises are concerned, however, it is clear that they should make ends meet by earning enough money to cover operating costs, depreciation and — perhaps — paying back interest on the capital invested in them by the state (I say 'perhaps' because the state might prefer that the organisation should rather reduce its price to the consumer than pay interest). Direct subsidies to state-sponsored bodies to cover trading losses are exceptional. In these cases the state decides that taking economic and social factors into consideration, those particular enterprises should be maintained.

11. The Judiciary

The Oireachtas makes laws,* the government enforces them; but laws can be unjust or even if just, unjustly enforced. The courts exist to decide cases in which the constitutionality of the laws is challenged and to ensure through judicial judgment that laws are fairly applied. In addition to deciding cases between individuals and the state, the courts decide issues between private citizens.

Judges deal with two different kinds of cases. First there are *criminal* cases, where a man or woman is charged with breaking a law (e.g. committing murder, robbing a bank, dangerous driving). Secondly there are *civil* cases where one person brings an action against another because of some injury done to him (e.g. slander, or money owed, or property rights violated).

Criminal Jurisdiction

A crime is an offence for which a person is liable to be punished — by death (e.g. in some cases of murder), imprisonment or a fine. Crimes vary in gravity and so the penalties attached to them vary.

The District Court

The Constitution provides that no person is to be tried on any criminal charge without a jury unless the offence is a minor one, a military one or one relating to emergency conditions. The district court justice, sitting without a jury, tries minor offences.

---

*The sources of Irish law are the common law (the customary law as laid down by the courts), the Oireachtas and the earlier parliaments — the Parliament of Ireland which ended with the Act of Union in 1800 and the Parliament of the United Kingdom of Great Britain and Ireland which ended with the Irish Free State (Agreement) Act, 1922.

The District Justice tries 'summary' offences (i.e. most minor offences) without a jury. The maximum term of imprisonment which may be imposed by a District Justice is twelve months. For many offences, the maximum term of imprisonment laid down by the relevant statute is less than this. The District Justice may also impose fines appropriate to summary offences. (Most road traffic offences are summary offences.) A person accused of certain more serious (i.e. 'indictable') offences may be tried summarily without a jury by a District Justice, provided that neither he nor the prosecution objects. For indictable offences for which this procedure is not or cannot be followed (which therefore must be tried before a judge and a jury), the District Justice conducts a preliminary examination of the case against the accused, using written statements of the evidence to be given by the witnesses for the prosecution, or, in certain circumstances, sworn depositions of the evidence of some or all of these witnesses. If he considers that there is a sufficient case to put the accused on trial for the offence or offences with which he has been charged, he sends the accused for trial either by the Circuit Court or (in the case of certain offences) by the Central Criminal Court. If he considers that there is not a sufficient case to put the accused on trial for any offence alleged, he discharges the accused as to that offence. Even if a District Justice has discharged the accused as to an offence, the prosecutor (now the Director of Public Prosecutions — see page 93), can nonetheless send the accused person forward for trial on that charge. The District Court consists of a President and thirty-four ordinary district justices. Eight justices, including the President, preside over Dublin cases. The rest of the country is divided into twenty-three districts and a DJ is assigned to preside over the sittings in each district. In addition there are nine movable justices.

The Circuit Court

Justice is administered in the Circuit Court by the President of that Court and eleven ordinary judges. The whole country is divided into eight areas called circuits and a judge is assigned to each of them. Four judges are assigned to the Dublin circuit. A jury consisting of twelve citizens listens to the evidence and decides whether the defendant is guilty or not. The judge's functions are to ensure that the trial is conducted properly, to decide questions of law, to sum up the evidence for the jury and to pass sentence. The Circuit Court can try all criminal cases that require a jury, except treason, murder, conspiracy to murder and — quaintly — piracy. Jurisdiction is exercised by the judge of the circuit in which the offence charged has been committed or in which the accused person has been arrested or resides. The Director of Public Prosecutions or the accused can apply to have a serious case sent forward to the Central Criminal Court. (This request might be made where a case has aroused such strong local feeling that the impartiality of a jury might be questionable.)

The Central Criminal Court

The President of the High Court nominates a judge or a number of judges from the High Court to act in the Central Criminal Court. Normally one judge (sitting with a jury) holds the court but the President can direct two or more judges to sit together for the purpose of a particular case. We have seen that some cases may be sent forward to this Court from the District Court and the Circuit Court. It is this Court that tries murder cases.

Special Criminal Courts

Under the Offences against the State Act, 1939, the government may establish a Special Criminal Court, when it is satisfied that the ordinary courts are inadequate to secure justice and public order. The court must have an uneven number of members (not less than three) appointed by the government. Since 1970, these have been existing or former judges. It sits without a jury.

Appeals

To the Circuit Court

Human judgment is fallible and consequently there is a system whereby appeal against court decisions can be made. An appeal can be made to the Circuit Court against a decision of the District Court. There is a re-hearing of the whole case. Fresh evidence can be called. The appeal is on the merits of the

case. If an allegation is made that the District Justice has conducted the case improperly or exceeded his powers, then the
appeal must be made to the High Court. The Circuit Court
(sitting without a jury) may confirm, vary or reverse the order
of a District Justice but not on the basis that it is bad *in form*.
The decision of the Circuit Court on appeal is final, except
that a question of law may be referred to the Supreme Court
for decision.

To the High Court

The High Court when appealed to from an inferior tribunal
has powers t review the orders or decisions of such a tribunal
from the point of view of *form*, that is to say, it decides whether
or not the lower court has exceeded its powers. In addition a
District Justice may ask the High Court to give a ruling on a
question of law: this is known as procedure by way of 'case
stated'.

To the Court of Criminal Appeal

A person convicted on indictment before the Central
Criminal Court, the Circuit Court or the Special Criminal
Court may appeal to the Court of Criminal Appeal. The Court
is normally constituted of three judges, one of them the Chief
Justice or a judge of the Supreme Court nominated by him,
and the others, two judges of the High Court. The convicted
person must obtain a certificate from the trial judge that his
case is suitable for appeal. If the trial judge refuses this, the
Court of Criminal Appeal itself will grant such leave if it feels
that a question of law is involved or that the trial has been
unsatisfactory. This Court has the power to affirm the convic-
tion, reverse it in whole or in part and reduce or increase the
sentence.

To the Supreme Court

If a point of law of exceptional public importance is involved
in a case brought before the Court of Criminal Appeal, the
appeal may be brought forward to the Supreme Court. The
Supreme Court consists of the Chief Justice and four other
judges.

Criminal Procedure

Where the District Justice has summary jurisdiction, i.e. in cases that he can decide by himself, proceedings begin when a 'complaint' or an 'information' is made (e.g. by a Garda) to the justice, to a peace commissioner or to the justice's clerk. This is followed by the issue of a District Court Summons which sets out the cause of the complaint and calls upon the defendant to attend before the Court to answer it. The summons must be served on the defendant in certain prescribed ways, otherwise it is invalid. When the case comes on for hearing, the justice hears the evidence on both sides, gives his decision and incorporates it in the order that he sets out in his minute book. In some cases the DJ may order the arrest of the defendant.

Prosecutions for indictable offences commence with a summons too. Only when the offence is serious is a warrant of arrest rather than a summons made out in the first instance. When the accused person appears before the District Court, a preliminary examination takes place. The accused is served with a statement of the charge and of the evidence intended to be adduced, with a list of witnesses and exhibits. At the hearing, either side may require any witness to be called and his evidence taken down in writing, read over, and signed by him. This sworn transcript of evidence is called a deposition. Witnesses called by one side may be cross-examined by the other. Finally, the accused, on being cautioned, may make a statement which is taken down in writing and may be used in evidence at his trial.

If, having heard submissions on both sides, the Justice is of opinion that the evidence is sufficient to put the accused on trial, he sends him forward to the Circuit Court or the Central Criminal Court either in custody or on bail. The justice generally can use his discretion on whether to allow bail or not; if he refuses, the accused can apply to the High Court to be admitted to bail. If he considers that there is not sufficient case against the accused, he discharges him.

When the accused has been returned for trial, the prosecution prepares the indictment — a written statement of the offence or offences with which he is charged. He is brought to court before judge and jury and pleads 'guilty' or 'not guilty' of the charge. The trial then proceeds with an opening statement by counsel for the prosecution, the calling of prosecution witnesses, examination and cross-examination followed by a hearing of the case for the defence in the same way. The accused may or may not elect to give evidence on his own behalf. Counsel on either side then sum up, the judge directs the jury on the law and reviews the evidence. The jury then retire to consider their verdict.

Civil Jurisdiction

There are two main classes of civil cases: (1) *contract*, where a person complains that another has broken an agreement, and (2) *tort*, where through a breach of legal duty by one person, another suffers some injury; an example of this is someone who throws a brick out of a window and injures a passerby. The thrower has a duty not to endanger others. In some cases the court may be asked to make an order forbidding a person from doing some wrongful act — for example a shopkeeper may ask the court to grant an injunction to prevent people who have no lawful interest in a dispute between himself and his employees from picketing his shop.

Civil proceedings are great in volume, diverse in kind. The most familiar cases are those in which a person seeks compensation for an injury, a person seeks payment of a debt, a will is disputed, ownership of land or property is contested, a person claims libel. The shelves of law libraries sag under the weight of people's outraged rights.

The District Court

This court has jurisdiction (1) in contract and tort where the claim does not exceed £250 (2) in ejectment for non-payment of rent where the rent does not exceed £315 per annum (3) in proceedings on behalf of the state, e.g. by a tax-collector, where the amount involved does not exceed £250. In addition it deals with intoxicating liquor licences, awards for maintenance to deserted wives and disputes concerning rent and hire purchase. A District Justice cannot decide actions for defamation, seduction, false imprisonment or malicious prosecution.

Civil proceedings in the District Court are begun by the issue and service of a document called a 'Civil Process'. Appeals are taken to the Circuit Court, where the action is re-heard. The decision of the Circuit Court in such an appeal is final on fact.

The Circuit Court

Unless all the interested parties to a suit consent, the jurisdiction of this court is confined to (1) actions in contract or tort where the claim does not exceed £2,000 (2) actions concerning the title to land when the valuation of the land does not exceed £100 (3) in equity suits (cases in which a person asks the court for an injunction or for some remedy other than payment of money), in probate matters (problems arising from wills) and suits for the administration of estates when the property or subject matter involved does not exceed £5,000 or the valuation of the land £100.

A Circuit Court Rules Committee (representing judges, barristers and solicitors) governs the practice and procedure of the Circuit Court. Proceedings commence with the drawing up of a Civil Bill by the plaintiff: this gives a simple statement of the plaintiff's claim. It is served on the defendant by a court official. The defendant thereupon files his defence, stating clearly the grounds on which he disputes the plaintiff's claim. The case is then pleaded in court. An appeal can be made to the High Court.

For hearing appeals from the Circuit Court the state is divided into a number of High Court Circuits and twice a year judges of the High Court sit in each county and county borough to hear such appeals. If the appeal is from Dublin Circuit Court or from a Circuit Court action with no oral evidence, it is heard by the High Court sitting in Dublin. Except where no oral evidence was heard in the Circuit Court, the appeal is by way of a complete re-hearing of the evidence. In a Circuit Court there is a right to have an action tried by a jury; the fact that the verdict of a Circuit Court jury may be set aside by a High Court judge, sitting alone, has tended to diminish the use of juries in these cases.

In hearing an appeal from a Circuit Court, a High Court judge may, on the application of either party in the case, state a case for the consideration of the Supreme Court on any question of law and he may adjourn the hearing until he gets such a ruling.

The High Court

The High Court consists of a President, nine ordinary judges and the President of the Circuit Court. The High Court can try all matters and cases of a civil nature no matter what part of the state they arise in or what amount is involved. The High Court can transfer to the Circuit Court cases that might have been commenced at the latter tribunal; and a plaintiff who might have commenced his proceedings in the Circuit Court but does so in the High Court may be awarded costs on the Circuit Court scale only.

Most of the steps taken by a plaintiff in the conduct of an action are carried out by his solicitor in consultation with counsel (a barrister). The first step is for the plaintiff to issue and serve on the defendant a 'Plenary Summons' which sets out what is claimed and why. The defendant, on getting the summons makes an 'appearance' in the appropriate office of the High Court. The plaintiff then sends the defendant a 'Statement of Claim' setting out in detail the allegations that he is making. The defendant responds with a 'Defence' which deals with each allegation in the Statement of Claim. To this the plaintiff may send a 'Reply'.

These documents do not deal with evidence; they are merely designed to clarify for each party the case that will arise in court. This pleading is under the control of the court through an officer called the Master of the High Court, with an appeal to a judge. Thus either party can get further and better particulars of any matter connected with the case, unless it is a question of evidence. When these steps have been taken, the pleadings are closed and the case is ready for trial. For some cases, e.g. a claim for a definite sum of money, a shorter form of procedure is followed. The plaintiff issues a 'Summary Summons' on which the amount of his claim is stated and the defendant is compelled to make his answer without further ado.

Proceedings in the High Court are tried in Dublin or by the judges of the High Court when the High Court on Circuit is travelling through the country to hear appeals from the Circuit Court.

In civil cases, the majority vote of nine of the twelve jurors sworn is sufficient to determine the verdict.

Civil Procedure

Most of the judgments which terminate actions are for the payment of money. Having got a favourable judgment, the plaintiff's next problem is to have it enforced. The principal way of getting paid is to have the property of the defendant seized and sold. An order is made to the County Registrar or in Dublin and Cork to the County or County Borough Sheriff, commanding him to levy the amount with interest and costs on the goods of the defendant. If the defendant fails to comply, the plaintiff may ask the District Court for an order directing that the amount due be paid by instalments. On this application the District Justice will examine the defendant as to his means in order to find out how much a week he can afford to pay. There are other remedies — for example, a person who owes money to the defendant may be directed to pay it to the plaintiff instead.

Only a small proportion of actions begun in the courts ever comes to trial at all: most are settled out of court. The rules of court are designed to foster such settlements. For instance in an action arising out of personal injuries sustained by a pedestrian in a motor accident, the pedestrian's legal advisers will try to settle the case by obtaining a payment sufficient to compensate him. If they fail, a summons will be issued and the pedestrian will indicate his resolution to pursue the claim. It is usual then for the defendant to pay into court a sum which he considers sufficient to satisfy the claim. The plaintiff can accept the sum offered and discontinue proceedings or go ahead with the action. This puts him in a dilemma. If he goes ahead with the action and obtains more damages than the amount lodged in court, he will get his costs in the ordinary way; if he gets less damages, then he must pay his own costs and the costs of the defendant after the date of the lodgment in court.

In motor accident cases the motorist will as a rule be insured against accident by an insurance company which then takes up the case on his behalf.

The Judges

From the figures already given, it will be seen that just over 60 judicial personages are engaged in carrying on the business of the courts in Ireland. All judges are appointed by the President on the advice of the government. There is a retirement age for all judges. They can be removed from office by the President 'for stated misbehaviour or incapacity' only on a resolution of both Houses of the Oireachtas. If they wish to resign they must send in a notice to the President. Judges are paid by the state.

The Attorney General

The Attorney General is head of the legal profession. We saw in an earlier chapter that he is the adviser to the government in matters of law and legal opinion, though he is not a member of the government. He is appointed by the government on the nomination of the Taoiseach (who may request his resignation). He retires from office with the Taoiseach. He may sue and be sued. In civil proceedings brought against the state, the Attorney General is joined with the state (Ireland) in a representative capacity as the law officer of state designated by the constitution. In his capacity as law officer of the state, the Attorney General nominates barristers as counsel to appear in the courts on his behalf and on behalf of the state, the government, government ministers and other authorities of the state acting in their official capacities. Other legal officers of the state are the Chief State Solicitor and his assistants and the State Solicitor for each county.

Article 30 of the Constitution provides that all crimes and offences prosecuted in any court constituted under Article 34 of the Constitution other than a court of summary jurisdiction shall be prosecuted in the name of the People and at the suit of the Attorney General or some other person authorised in accordance with law to act for that purpose. The Prosecution of Offences Act, 1974, created the office of Director of Public Prosecutions and conferred on him authority, within the meaning of Article 30 of the Constitution, to prosecute in the name of the People of Ireland.

Barristers

Barristers are known collectively as 'the Bar' and also collectively (or individually) as counsel. It is their privilege to plead cases before the higher courts. They are divided into two groups, senior counsel and junior counsel. The admission of persons to the Bar is regulated by a society called the Benchers of King's Inns. All candidates for call to the bar are required to become students of King's Inns. There they attend a course of lectures in the theory and practice of law and dine in common. The full period of study is four years but this may be shortened in the case of persons who possess a degree in Law. In addition, candidates must attend certain law courses in a university. Having passed the final examination (and eaten the required number of dinners) the student is duly called to the bar and authorised to appear in any court in the state. It is customary for the newly called barrister to spend some time as a pupil to a practising barrister. A pupil is called a 'devil'. Many of those who are called to the bar do not practise but find employment in industry or the public service. The Benchers of King's Inns hold discipline over the profession.

The Solicitors

The scope of the solicitor's work is very broad and it increases with the increase in legislation. Take one segment of their interest alone — property. Title to land and property must be shown by legal documents (deeds) and so the solicitor generally has a part to play in the buying and selling of all land and buildings. There are laws to regulate the leasing of property, the building of property, the demolition of property. On these and many other matters, legal issues can arise, e.g. can a landlord raise the rent? Can a tenant demand repairs? Can a man put a window into his house looking on to his neighbour's backyard? Can he put petrol-pumps on the public pavement? Can he build a dance hall in a residential area? Or beside a hospital? The solicitor's services are needed on such issues by private and commercial interests. The Town Planning Act which was passed in 1963 complicates property matters still further. Other general areas in which solicitors help in the administration of law are in the making of wills, in company law, in taxation law, in traffic law. The other part of the solicitor's work is preparing cases for litigation. He can appear as advocate for his clients in any court. In the Higher Courts, he generally arranges for counsel for his clients, helps counsel in practical matters such as preparing the evidence, arranges for the appearance of witnesses and he acts as intermediary between counsel and clients.

The Incorporated Law Society of Ireland is the statutory body which controls the solicitor's profession. It keeps a roll of solicitors. At present there are about 2,000 on the roll. A committee of the Incorporated Law Society can investigate allegations made against any solicitor and, in a proper case, it can refer the matter to the President of the High Court, who can deal with it either by removing the offender's name from the roll of solicitors (thus preventing him from practising) or otherwise, e.g. by compelling him to make good, out of his own pocket, costs incurred by a client through the solicitor's negligence. The power to restore a name to the roll is also vested in the High Court. The Incorporated Law Society maintains an Indemnity Fund out of which clients who suffer loss owing to their solicitor's dishonesty are compensated.

Admission to the profession of solicitor is based on a combination of practical training as an apprentice and examinations. The period of apprenticeship is five years although this is reduced in the case of graduates in Law. Courses of lectures are provided by the Incorporated Law Society. These are compulsory. There are three examinations before admission to practice.

The Jury

The county registrar in each county keeps a Jury List which comprises the names of local government electors who are twenty-one years or more. All these people are liable to be called to serve on juries. Unless they are excused by the court, e.g. on a doctor's certificate, people called to serve on juries must serve, otherwise they are fined. A jury consists of twelve people. In criminal cases they must arrive at an unanimous verdict. If, having been called three times by a judge they fail on each occasion to voice such a verdict, they are dismissed and a new trial is ordered.

Court Sittings

The legal year (those parts of the year during which judges sit in court) is divided into four 'sittings' — Hilary (12 January-31 March), Easter (15 April-18 May), Trinity (1 June-31 July), and Michaelmas (12 October-21 December).

Officers of the Courts

In the High Court there is a Central Office under the control of an official called the Master of the High Court which makes most of the arrangements for the orderly conduct of business in that court. County Registrars take care of the administrative work of the Circuit Court. In Dublin County and County Borough and Cork County and County Borough there are sheriffs; elsewhere the functions of sheriffs have been transferred to the County Registrars. In the District Court, District Court Clerks do the administrative work.

The Finances of the Law

The burden of supporting the courts falls mainly on public funds. The administration of the criminal law is a public charge. In the civil courts, however, the litigant has to make a substantial contribution to the cost of his action.

He has to pay the appropriate court fees, bear the expense of collecting evidence and bringing his witnesses to court, pay the fees of his solicitor and counsel. Though judges are paid by the state, the court fees are set at such a figure that the wages and pensions of the court officials and the provision and maintenance of buildings and equipment can be paid for out of them. On the civil side, where the state is involved it is of course the state that has to pay costs if unsuccessful.

Costs

'Costs' describes all the expenses of litigation that one party has to pay to the other. Any party to an action has to pay his own solicitor all the solicitor's proper fees and expenses for acting according to the client's express or implied instructions. These are called 'solicitor and client costs'.

The costs that the loser has to pay to the successful party are not his actual costs and expenses but only such as have been 'necessarily or properly incurred' for the conduct of the case. In practice, each side will have spent more than was necessary, because they will have thought it prudent to be prepared for any eventuality in the course of the trial. The winner's solicitor sends a bill of costs to the loser's solicitor. If it is agreed, it is paid forthwith; if it is disputed it is brought before a court official called the Taxing Master who gives a hearing at which each disputed item is discussed and allowed or disallowed by him. There is an appeal to a judge of the High Court. When the taxation is completed, the sum allowed is called 'party and party costs'. In cases settled out of court, costs are normally agreed upon; if they are not, they can be brought before the Taxing Master. A client who thinks his solicitor is overcharging him can have his costs taxed too. The taxation of a bill of costs involves more costs. If less than one-sixth of the bill is disallowed, the challenger pays the cost of the taxation; if more, the party claiming the bill pays the cost.

The costs which a solicitor may lawfully charge are largely regulated by law. For work in the courts, they are regulated by the Rules of Court. For work outside of the courts, a scale of charges is laid down. For example, in property dealings (including house purchase) he will get a certain proportion of the purchase price of the property.

The fees of members of the bar are not regulated by law. The profession itself prescribes minimum fees, but a barrister will charge such a fee as he feels his services are worth. The barrister gets fees for various services, e.g. 'refresher' fees if the case lasts more than a specified time or a fee paid for consultation with the client; but the greatest part of the fees paid to him is accounted for by the 'fee on brief' — the lump sum payable to him for preparing and conducting the case. It is the etiquette of the bar that if a senior counsel appears, a junior counsel will appear also (except he appears for an accused person on indictment). The fee paid to a junior counsel is two-thirds that of the senior's fee. The solicitor employs the counsel and pays him the fee agreed upon even though later, in taxation, that fee may be disallowed. A barrister cannot sue for his fees.

When a man brings an action and succeeds, being awarded his claim with costs, the 'costs' awarded him will be considerably less than his actual costs. This can affect settlements out of court. Thus X may claim £1,000 damages from Y and Y may think that £1,000 is a fair estimate of his liability. But he may offer only £900 in settlement, knowing that X will probably realise that it is better to get £900 in settlement than to get a judgment for £1,000 and have to pay out, say, £150 over and above what he can recover in costs from Y.

Legal Aid

Litigation costs money. Can the poor person then get justice? On the criminal side, the Criminal Justice (Legal Aid) Act, 1962, ensures that a person charged on a serious indictable offence will have, at state expense, all the legal advice and advocacy that he needs. On the civil side, there is no state aid for the poor litigant except in state side proceedings.

However, various social, charitable and religious bodies have occasionally obtained the free services of solicitors and, where necessary, counsel, to assist poor persons. Many actions brought in the higher courts are for damages for injuries sustained in road and factory accidents. Very few of these plaintiffs have the means of paying the costs of such an action. Some depend on the help of their trade union, some are insured against claims being made against them, but many of them rely on the goodwill of the legal profession.

12. The Garda Síochána

Crime prevention, crime detection, court service and traffic control are the main functions of the Gardaí. The Garda must have a considerable knowledge of civil and criminal law and of court procedures to carry out his work. The Gardaí provide a variety of other services too. They help the Central Statistics Office in the collection of agricultural statistics and the general census of population. They enforce the Weights and Measures Acts, the gun-licensing laws, and the Aliens Act. They provide protection for the President, members of the government, members of the diplomatic corps, embassies and visiting heads of state.

Background
In 1822 an Act was passed establishing four provincial police forces in Ireland. Before that the only police forces were watchmen employed by the local authorities in the larger towns, and barony constables in the rural areas. In 1836 the four police forces were amalgamated to form the Irish Constabulary which policed all the country save Dublin City. Dublin City was policed by a separate force — the Dublin Metropolitan Police. The Irish Constabulary was re-styled the Royal Irish Constabulary for its part in the suppression of the Fenians. In 1922 the native administration took over the existing police structure and what was the RIC became the Civic Guard. In 1925 the DMP was integrated with the rest of the Garda Síochána.

Organisation
The Garda Síochána is a national, unarmed police force under central control with administrative headquarters situated in the Phoenix Park, Dublin. A Commissioner

99

appointed by the government and responsible to the Minister for Justice is at the head of the force. To assist him he has two Deputy Commissioners and four Assistant Commissioners.

Outside the Dublin Metropolitan Area (which comprises Dublin City and County as well as portions of Meath, Kildare and Wicklow) the country is divided into nineteen divisions. For the most part, divisions correspond in area to counties but some adjoining counties have been grouped together to form one unit. Each division is divided into districts (about five to each) and each district into sub-districts (about seven to each). The Dublin Metropolitan Area is under the control of a Deputy or Assistant Commissioner having his headquarters at Dublin Castle. The area is divided into four divisions, each under the control of a Chief Superintendent while a fifth Chief Superintendent is in charge of crime for the whole area.

A Chief Superintendent is in charge of each division and a Superintendent in charge of each district. The smallest unit consists of the sergeant with his party of guards controlling a sub-district and the strength throughout the rural areas is usually about 1 sergeant and 2 or 3 guards.

The Inspector rank is only indirectly a link in the chain of responsibility. His function is mainly supervisory except when the Superintendent is absent on leave or through illness in which case the Inspector takes charge of the district. Some of the big Dublin City stations are under the direct control of an Inspector.

At headquarters there are five main departments each under the control of a Deputy or Assistant Commissioner.

In 1978 the strength of the force was:

Chief Supt.	Supt.	Insp.	Stn. Sgt.	Sgt.	Gardaí	Total
39	141	204	3	1,553	7,263 =	9,203

(These figures include 5 Ban/Sgts. and 52 Ban/Gardaí)

Recruitment

Men and women are recruited between the ages of nineteen and twenty-six. Men must be at least 5ft 9in. in height and women at least 5ft 5in.

Entrance examinations are conducted by the Civil Service Commissioners and successful candidates are placed on a list in the order of merit. In this order, candidates are called for medical examination, oral Irish test and an interview before a board of officers. If successful, they are then called for appointment to the force. An average of 330 a year has been recruited for the past ten years.

Training covers a period of 22 weeks, and every recruit is on probation for a period of two years from his date of appointment. Failure to attain a good standard of efficiency within this period may mean his discharge from the force. The training centre is situated at Templemore, Co. Tipperary, and is under the control of a Chief Superintendent.

Detective Force

A Technical Bureau is provided to assist detectives in the scientific investigation of crime. It is divided into the following sections: Records of Criminals, Fingerprint Section, Mapping Section, Photographic Section, Ballistic Section, Investigation Section.

Interpol

Interpol (the International Criminal Police Organisation) which, founded in 1923 with headquarters in Vienna, had collapsed with the imminence of World War II in 1938, was re-established in 1945 with headquarters in Paris. It is not, as some detective films imply, a sort of supranational police force. It is an organisation that provides the means for international criminal police co-operation. About 80 countries are affiliated to the organisation (Ireland was affiliated in 1947). Each member country has a national central bureau which channels requests for information or help to the Central Bureau in Paris which in turn transmits the requests to the relevant national bureau abroad. That bureau then contacts the local police that can deal with the requests.

13. The Defence Forces

Our present defence forces consist of the permanent defence force and the reserve defence force, both comprising army, navy and air components. The supreme command of the defence forces is vested in the President by the Constitution. All commissioned officers of the defence forces hold their commissions from the President. However, actual control over all military affairs is, broadly speaking, exercised by the government, and, in particular, by the Minister for Defence.

A Council of Defence aids and counsels the Minister for Defence on all matters in relation to the business of the Department of Defence on which the Minister may consult it. The council consists of two civil members, namely the Minister of State at the Department of Defence, and the Secretary of the Department of Defence, and three military members, namely the Chief of Staff, the Adjutant-General and the Quartermaster-General.

The Chief of Staff, the Adjutant-General and the Quartermaster-General of the defence forces, who must be officers of the Permanent Defence Force, are appointed by the President. Their term of office must not exceed five years but they are eligible for re-appointment. They head respectively the three principal military branches of the Department of Defence, namely the branch of the Chief of Staff, the branch of the Adjutant-General and the branch of the Quartermaster-General. The Minister for Defence has assigned certain duties in connection with the business of the Department of Defence to each of these officers and each of them is directly responsible to the minister for the performance of those duties. The minister has delegated to the Chief of Staff the co-ordination of the business of the three branches.

For the purpose of military administration the country is divided into four territorial Commands — known as the Eastern, Southern, Western and Curragh Commands. The Minister for Defence has delegated, with certain exceptions, the command of the defence forces within these boundaries to the respective Officers Commanding Commands.

A Judge Advocate General, who must be a practising barrister-at-law but must not be a member of the defence forces, is appointed by the President to perform such duties as the government may from time to time assign to him. Broadly his duties relate to the review of the findings of courts-martial and other military courts to ensure the legality of the proceedings and findings (including punishments awarded).

The permanent defence force includes the Air Corps, the Naval Service and the Army Nursing Service. The establishments of the force provide for approximately 16,500 all ranks and the present strength is approximately 14,000 all ranks. The reserve defence force consists of approximately 20,000 all ranks and is divided into the First Line Reserve, An Fórsa Cosanta Áitiúil and An Slua Muirí.

The following are the service corps of the defence forces:

Infantry Corps
Artillery Corps
Cavalry Corps
Corps of Engineers
Signal Corps
Ordnance Corps
Supply and Transport Corps
Medical Corps
Military Police Corps
Air Corps
Naval Service
Army School of Music
Observer Corps

The branches of the Chief of Staff, the Adjutant-General and the Quartermaster-General and the offices of the directors of the various corps are located in Dublin. The headquarters of the Eastern, Southern, Western and Curragh Commands are in Dublin, Cork, Athlone and the Curragh respectively. The training depots of the majority of the Corps are located in the

Curragh Training Camp as is also the Military College.

Special military establishments include the Military College, the Army Equitation School at McKee Barracks, Dublin, the Army School of Music at Cathal Brugha Barracks, Dublin, and the Army Apprentice School at Naas. The last-named establishment trains apprentices to various trades.

All recruitment to the defence forces is on a voluntary basis. Officers are recruited through the medium of cadetships, except in the case of certain professional officers (e.g. doctors) who must have appropriate qualifications and who are appointed to be officers on recruitment. Suitably qualified NCOs can obtain commissions by undergoing a Potential Officer's Course of one year's duration at the Military College. Cadets undergo a course of training, which normally lasts two years, before being appointed officers. Officers serve until they retire, resign or are dismissed by the President as the case may be. Men (including non-commissioned officers) enlisted in the defence forces serve until discharged for any of the various prescribed reasons. The normal minimum term of enlistment in the permanent defence force is three years (four years in the case of the naval service).

The Air Corps

Organisation and establishments

The air corps comprises Air Corps Headquarters which commands and controls an administrative wing, a technical wing, a flying wing and a fighter control unit. Its present establishments provide for approximately 800 all ranks.

Location

The air corps maintains two main stations: (1) at Baldonnel where the headquarters of the corps and the greater part of the technical and administrative services which maintain the corps are situated. Baldonnel is also the centre for advanced flying training including helicopter training and technical training; (2) at Gormanston where the Basic Flying Training School and the essential administrative and servicing personnel to maintain it are situated.

Training

The corps trains pilots and technicians. The method of pilot intake has varied from time to time. Short service schemes and schemes whereby the air corps accepted, as trainee pilots, commissioned officers who had completed the two-year cadet course in the Military College have been used in the past. Currently the corps recruits and trains its own cadets who also undergo periods of military training at the Military College during their cadetship. Pilot training is, of course, continuous but the formal instruction in basic and advanced training courses occupies about two years, after which the pilot qualifies as a military pilot and qualifies for a commercial pilot's licence.

Aeronautical Engineers

The air corps recruits engineers direct from civilian life. Ordinarily, they are Bachelors of Electrical Engineering and/or Mechanical Engineering. On being commissioned they undergo an initial 10-week course at the Military College and are then sent to aircraft factories abroad for 6-9 month courses in aircraft engines, air-frames, electronics or armament, as appropriate.

Technicians

Technicians for the corps are recruited through an apprentice scheme. The training is designed to produce first-class technicians. The normal apprenticeship period is five years.

Apart from its military functions, the air corps has played and continues to play an important role in the economic life of the state. The air corps provided a valuable nucleus of trained pilots and technicians to assist in the establishment of Aer Lingus. A feature of the development of Aer Lingus has been the continuous support received by it from the corps by way of trained pilots from the regular officers of the corps and through the various short service pilot training schemes. It is also a continuous source of supply for trained technicians and specialists for Aer Lingus. The air corps provides assistance to other government departments and state bodies in a variety of ways, e.g. flight testing of navigational aids at the commercial airports, assistance in training of air traffic control staffs, advice and assistance in air safety procedures, aerial photography, air search and rescue, air ambulance missions and fishing protection patrols.

The Naval Service

The Naval Service is a branch of the defence forces. It consists of a Naval Headquarters located at the Department of Defence, Dublin, and a naval base and dockyard at Haulbowline, Co. Cork. The vessels of the naval service comprise two all-weather patrol vessels, three coastal minesweepers and one general purpose vessel. A third all-weather patrol vessel is expected to come into service in mid 1979 and a fourth in 1980. In addition to the regular service personnel it has a 1st Line Reserve component and a Voluntary Reserve (An Slua Muirí).

The main functions of the naval service in peace-time include coastal patrol, fishery protection, co-operation in air/sea rescue, aid to the civil power in the sea areas in which the state enjoys sovereign rights. The naval base at Haulbowline provides for the needs of our naval vessels including the supply of trained personnel, stores and fuel, and dockyard facilities.

An Slua Muirí

An Slua Muirí is a reserve element of the naval service. It is organised in five companies which are based at the principal seaports. The function of these companies is to provide for port control and seaward defence of the harbours concerned.

The Military College

The Military College, established in the late twenties, is the principal military educational institution. Located in Pearse Barracks, Curragh Training Camp, it consists of three separate schools, namely the Cadet School, the Infantry School and the Command and Staff School. Each school has its own staff of instructors in non-specialist subjects. Specialist officer instructors are attached to the college from their own corps, their instructional services being available to all three schools.

The Cadet School

The purpose of the school is to develop character and to provide training in military and academic subjects in order to enable cadets to enter upon their duties as officers in the non-specialist corps of the defence forces. The course of training which lasts two years is also designed to foster and encourage initiative and to develop qualities of leadership.

Following consideration of the recommendation of the Commission on Higher Education that the training of military cadets should be associated with university studies, the Minister for Defence decided in August 1969 that appropriately qualified members of the cadet class who were appointed in 1968, should be given the opportunity of pursuing university studies at University College, Galway. A total of 14 Cadets commenced courses in Arts, Commerce, Science or Engineering in October 1969. Since then appropriately qualified members of each cadet class appointed have been given the opportunity to undergo university studies at UCG and approximately one hundred and forty officers have been conferred with degrees. Similar facilities will be provided for members of future cadet classes. The cost of college and examination fees as well as text books is being met from the Vote for Defence.

Spiritual instruction, games and sports are an integral part of the curriculum. Extra-curricular activities are wide and varied and include debating societies and camera and record clubs, a parachute club and several adventure sports clubs affiliated to the Association for Adventure Sports. The cadet school has its own library and full use is made of the first class swimming pool, the riding school and other installations in the Curragh Camp.

The Infantry School

The school has been in existence since 1930. As the name implies, it is primarily concerned with the continuation training of infantry officers. It provides a variety of courses in infantry weapons, in nuclear, biological and chemical (NBC) warfare and in junior leadership. Its main function, however, is to conduct a standard course (duration 4 months) for infantry officers to fit them for command of infantry sub-units. The broad scope of the course attracts nominations from corps other than infantry. Graduation on the course is an essential qualification for promotion in the infantry corps. Instruction on the course is through the medium of Irish and the course is almost exclusively military in character.

The Command and Staff School

The principal function of the command and staff school is to conduct, command and staff courses for military officers irrespective of their corps. The course is of approximately nine months duration and its main aim is to fit officers to hold senior appointments in the rank of commandant and upwards, either in the capacity of commanders or as staff officers. Graduation on the course is an essential qualification for promotion from junior to senior rank.

The course is mainly military in character and is concerned with military history, supply and movement, military tactics, nuclear warfare, civil defence and staff duties. With regard to the latter, a great deal of the subject matter is analogous to similar studies in the commercial and industrial spheres.

There are many lectures by visiting representatives of industrial, transport and government agencies whose activities impinge on military matters. A main feature of the course is the development in its students of a clear and logical approach to the appreciation and solving of problems.

Further Training

The command and staff course is not the final phase of the formal planned training programme for the military officer. The military college conducts seminars, study periods, demonstrations and short courses covering current developments and new techniques for senior officers of the forces.

Training of Foreign Military Personnel

At the request of the Zambian authorities the training of personnel of the Zambian Army was undertaken at the Military College. The first training course provided was for six Zambian cadets from October 1967 to June 1969.

These courses followed, generally, the syllabus of training for Irish cadets and were designed to fit the cadets for commissioned rank. Tuition was of necessity imparted in the English language. However, as much as possible of general training, e.g. parades, visits to institutions and industries, games, etc., was common to both Irish and Zambian cadets.

A training course, at the Infantry School, was also provided for six Zambian Infantry Officers from February to July 1969.

External Service

From July 1960 to June 1964 Irish troops formed part of ONUC, the United Nations Force in the Congo (now Zaire) — which from January 1961 to March 1962 was under an Irish Commander. From April 1964 to October 1973 Irish troops formed part of the United Nations Force in Cyprus (UNFICYP) where a small number of Irish Army personnel which includes the Force Commander are at present serving with UN Headquarters. Between October 1973 and May 1974 two Irish Infantry Groups served in the Middle East as part of the United Nations Emergency Force (UNEF) which was established after the Arab/Israeli War in October 1973. Since 1958, Irish officers have been attached to the United Nations Truce Supervision Organisation (UNTSO) in the Middle East where at present approximately 20 Irish officers are serving. Since June 1978 Irish troops have formed part of the United Nations Interim Force in Lebanon (UNIFIL) at Battalion strength as well as at Force Headquarters. Irish officers have also served with the United Nations in the Lebanon, on the India/Pakistan border and in Dutch New Guinea.

Civil Defence

The purpose of Civil Defence is to save life and property in time of war. The Oireachtas has placed the duty of organising it on the various local authorities acting under the direction and guidance of the Minister for Defence. Each local authority has a plan to meet the requirements of its area in regard to warden, rescue, casualty, fire-fighting and welfare services. The organisation depends on trained volunteers. Volunteers attend training for about two hours a week during the autumn, winter and spring months. Men and women of eighteen years of age and upwards may enrol. Recruiting started in 1956. At the beginning of 1978 there were approximately 30,000 members.

14. The Government of Northern Ireland

Under the Government of Ireland Act, 1920, Northern Ireland, while remaining part of the United Kingdom, was given a measure of control over local affairs. This control was exercised by a parliament consisting of two Houses — a House of Commons and a Senate — and a government composed of a Prime Minister and a small cabinet of ministers. Only about ten per cent of the revenue of Northern Ireland came under the direct control of the Northern Ireland government, the bulk of it being collected by the UK government. To represent it at Westminster Northern Ireland elected twelve members. A large part of the general legislation of the UK Parliament applied and still does to Northern Ireland in the same way as to other parts of the kingdom. In March 1972 an Act was passed at Westminster transferring for one year to a Secretary of State for Northern Ireland and the United Kingdom Parliament the legislative and executive powers formerly vested in the Northern Ireland government and parliament. This legislation was renewed for a further year.

The Northern Ireland Constitution Act, 1973, provided for a seventy-eight member Assembly, elected by a system of proportional representation, which would decide how best to set up a power-sharing Executive. In May 1974 the Executive collapsed and other provision had to be made urgently for the government of Northern Ireland. Under the 1973 Act the powers devolved since 1 January 1974 to the Assembly and Executive did not automatically revert to the Westminster Parliament and the UK government. However, the Act enabled the Assembly to be prorogued in certain circumstances.

On 29 May 1974 the Assembly was prorogued for a period of

four months. In July 1974 the Northern Ireland Constitution Act, 1974, became law. It provided for temporary arrangements for the government of Northern Ireland by the Secretary of State for Northern Ireland and also provided for the holding of a Constitutional Convention, the elections for which took place on 1 May 1975. The Convention submitted a report to the Secretary of State on 7 November 1975 and was recommenced from 3 February 1976. It was dissolved on 5 March 1976 without any further report having been made. Direct rule was renewed.

Representation at Westminster

Twelve members are returned by Northern Ireland constituencies to the House of Commons at Westminster. It is proposed to increase the number to at least sixteen but no more than eighteen.

Civil Service

Northern Ireland Office

At present the Secretary of State for Northern Ireland directs, through the Northern Ireland Office, the work of the Northern Ireland departments. He has the help of two ministers of state and two parliamentary secretaries of state. His office also deals with the reserved matters, particularly in the law and order field — courts, prisons, control of firearms and explosives, civil defence, elections.

The civil service of Northern Ireland is in general organised on the lines of the civil service in Britain.

Department of the Civil Service

The new Department of the Civil Service is responsible for personnel management including recruitment, training, promotion, pay, pensions and conditions of service in the civil service and for the co-ordination of pay policies in the public sector as a whole.

The Department of the Civil Service also provides the staff for the civil service commission which is an independent body responsible for the recruitment of all non-industrial staff for the Northern Ireland civil service.

Department of Finance

Treasury Group: Exercises financial control of Northern Ireland departments for the purpose of presentation of Parliamentary Estimates, the annual Public Expenditure Surveys and Cash Limits; the investment of public funds; government borrowing, stock issues and Treasury Bills; the submission of Estimates and Financial Statements and the examination of legislative proposals from the financial aspect.

Central Economic Service: Provides an economic, statistical and social research service to all Northern Ireland departments supplementing where appropriate departmental services. Publishes statistics relating to Northern Ireland.

Departmental Group: Works and Buildings for Northern Ireland departments and some UK departments in Northern Ireland; valuation and rating (including rate collection); Land Registry; Registry of Deeds; Registrar General; Census; Public Record Office.

The Office of Legislative Draftsman is attached to the department.

Public Record Office: The record office is concerned with the reception and control of the records of government departments, courts of law and all other public bodies over which the government of Northern Ireland has power to legislate. In addition it acquires on an extensive scale private documents of historical, economic or social significance.

Valuation Office: This office makes and revises the valuation of property for rating purposes; it also advises the Board of Inland Revenue on property valuations in connection with income tax, capital transfer tax, capital gains tax and development land tax.

Department of Commerce

The primary responsibility of this department is the development of the trade and industry of Northern Ireland. A major part of the department's resources and efforts are directed towards promoting expansion by existing industry and attracting new industry into Northern Ireland; other functions include energy supply and conservation; the development of tourism; consumer protection (including weights and measures); registration of companies and export promotion.

Department of Manpower Services
This department has responsibility for the administration of government policy in relation to the employment and training of labour.

It operates twenty-seven employment service offices across the province as well as a network of careers offices; administers a training programme including fourteen government Training Centres and runs a Youth Opportunities Programme designed to provide 6,000 training and work experience places for young people.

Department of Education
Public education in Northern Ireland, apart from higher education, is administered centrally by the Department of Education and at local level by five area boards — known as Education and Library Boards.

In the field of higher education the department is the main provider of finance for the two universities. It also discharges most of the functions of the former Department of Community Relations (amalgamated with the department on 1 April 1975) which include responsibility for formulating and sponsoring policies for the improvement of community relations in Northern Ireland.

Department of Health and Social Services
This department is responsible for the provision of all health and personal social welfare services.

Department of the Environment
This department is responsible for: housing policy; regional strategy; development plans; construction and maintenance of roads and bridges; provision of water supply and sewerage services; local government (general supervision of administrative and financial matters); and other environmental and amenity services.

Department of Agriculture
The Department of Agriculture is responsible for the development of agricultural, forestry and fishing industries; collection of agricultural census data and compilation of statistics; advisory services to all farmers; agricultural research, education and training.

Office of N.I. Parliamentary Commissioner for Administration and Office of the N.I. Commissioner for Complaints
The Commissioner examines complaints from members of the public who claim to have suffered injustice in consequence of maladministration.

Local Government

The reorganisation of local government and other services took effect on 1 October 1973. The following is a summary of the new provisions:
Local Services: The new district councils have direct control of a wide range of local services, in addition to their consultative and representative functions.
Roads and Water and Sewerage Services: These are administered by the Department of the Environment (NI) which has a chain of local offices.
Planning: Is administered by the Department of the Environment and operates through six divisional offices.

The District Councils
The district councils have three main roles:
1. *A Direct Role:* The councils are directly responsible for a range of local services including: gas supplies and the management of gasworks; local tourist development schemes; local harbour administration; enforcement of building control regulation; entertainment, culture and recreation, including provision of public parks and open spaces, local museums, swimming baths and sport and recreation centres; clean air, and certain aspects of food hygiene; burial grounds, mortuaries and crematoria; cleansing and sanitation, including domestic and trade refuse collection, street cleansing, removal of derelict motor vehicles, and litter prevention, public toilets and rodent and pest control; caravan sites and site licences;

licences for such purposes as pleasure boats, hoardings, cinemas, storage of petroleum spirit, public entertainment and street trading.

2. *A Representative Role:* They send forward locally elected representatives to sit as members of statutory boards and other bodies. These include — education and library boards, health and social services boards, Northern Ireland Housing Council and executive, Northern Ireland fire authority, electricity consumers' council, drainage council for Northern Ireland, the sports council.

3. *A Consultative Role:* Certain government departments and agencies directly responsible for regional services are required by law to consult the district councils to obtain the views of the local people on the operation of those services in the various districts.

15. International Organisations

Just as the citizen, to advance or maintain his interests and ideals, joins various organisations, so Ireland as a state is a member of many international organisations. There follows a brief outline of a number of the more important international organisations. Though these impinge on our interest we are not members of all of them.

The European Communities

There are three European Communities — the European Coal and Steel Community (ECSC), the European Atomic Energy Community (Euratom), and the European Economic Community (EEC or Common Market). The three Communities have the same nine member countries and operate through the same institutions — the Council of Ministers, the Commission, the European Parliament and the Court of Justice. Because of this their identities tend to merge and people often refer to 'the European Community' rather than 'the European Communities'.

There were many factors leading to the establishment of the European Communities after the second World War. However, the basic drive was a desire to create close economic and political unity between the countries of Western Europe, particularly France and Germany. In this way it was hoped to prevent the outbreak of further war in the area.

The first Community was established in 1952 when six countries — Belgium, France, Germany, Italy, Luxembourg and the Netherlands — agreed to pool their coal and steel production under a single authority. Following the success of this experiment in co-operation, the Six created, by treaties signed in Rome in 1957, the European Economic Community (EEC) and the European Atomic Energy Community (Euratom). Euratom brought co-operation in the peaceful application of nuclear energy, the EEC created a Common Market (it removed by stages all trade barriers between member countries and erected a common tariff wall around the Community) and the means of promoting throughout the Community 'a harmonious development of economic activities, a continuous and balanced expansion, an increase in stability, an accelerated raising of the standard of living, and closer relations between the states belonging to it'.

In January 1973 Ireland, along with Britain and Denmark, became a member of the three Communities.

Community Institutions

The *Council of Ministers* and the *European Commission* are the key policy-making bodies of the Communities. Each of the nine member governments is represented on the Council of Ministers. The Council makes the major policy decisions. Actual attendance at a Council session varies according to the subject to be discussed: finance Ministers meet on economic, monetary and financial matters, agricultural Ministers on farm policy and so on. Commission members attend Council meetings but they have no vote.

The Commission, which has its headquarters in Brussels, comprises thirteen members. They are appointed by unanimous agreement of the nine governments. They take an oath to perform their duties with complete independence and may neither seek nor accept instructions from any government. They have under them officials divided into departments called directorates-general. Each directorate-general deals with some aspects of the Communities' work, e.g. industrial and technological affairs, competition, agriculture, social affairs. The Commissioners divide out responsibility for the various directorates-general among themselves. They take decisions by majority vote. Decisions once made are presented as the view of all the Commissioners. The Commission alone has the vital power to propose legislation and to draw up policies, and, once the Council has agreed to them, it implements them; and it makes sure that the Communities' treaties and laws are applied.

The *European Parliament*, which meets in Luxembourg or

Strasbourg, has (from June 1979) 410 members elected directly by the citizens of the member states. France, Germany, Italy and the UK each elect 81 members, the Netherlands elects 25 members, Belgium 24, Denmark 16, Ireland 15 and Luxembourg 6. The 15 Irish members are elected from 4 constituencies — Dublin city (4), Leinster apart from Dublin city (3), Munster (5), Connaught-Ulster (3). Members, however, do not sit according to nationality but in multi-national political groupings. The European Parliament brings a measure of democratic pressure to bear on the workings of the Community. The European Parliament has some control over the Commission, for instance, through the use of Question Time. Each year the Commission publishes a report on the past year's activities for debate by the Parliament; furthermore the President of the Commission each year presents a programme of future activity to the Parliament. This procedure allows the Parliament to criticise past activities and comment on future policies. Parliament also has power to remove the Commission on a motion of censure carried by a two-thirds majority. Parliament is consulted on a great number of legislative proposals but the Community's budget, which is prepared by the Commission, is effectively controlled by the Council, though the Parliament now has power to increase some parts of the budget. The Council, like the Commission, participates in the debates of the Parliament.

The *Court of Justice of the European Communities* (the 'European Court'), which sits in Luxembourg, is composed of nine judges chosen from among nationals of the member states by common consent of the nine Governments. The Court hears cases between member states where a breach of the Treaties is alleged; it judges what the respective rights and obligations of the Community institutions and the institutions of the member states are; it can review the decisions of public authorities where misuse of power, violation of the treaties, bad procedure or lack of competence are alleged; it can decide points of law in cases brought by individuals and organisations for any alleged damages by Community institutions or their servants in the performance of their duties; finally it can act as a Court of Appeal in cases where the Commission fines industrial or commercial undertakings for infringing certain treaty rules. For the enforcement of judgments against individuals or private companies the Court relies on the law enforcement agencies of the member states; for the enforcement of judgments against member states the Court relies in practice on voluntary compliance, and indeed no government has ignored the judgments of the Court.

The *European Investment Bank* is the Communities' long-term finance institution. It lends on a non-profit basis for investment projects promoting regional development, industrial modernisation and transnational Community projects. It also provides EEC development finance in many third world countries.

The United Nations

The United Nations was founded in 1945 when fifty countries signed the Charter which had been presented to the United Nations Conference on International Affairs held at San Francisco that year. The Charter was based largely on the proposals which the US, UK, USSR and China had worked out at discussions held in 1944 at Dumbarton Oaks (Washington, D.C.).

The objects of the UN are to maintain international peace and security and to co-operate in bringing about the political, economic and social conditions necessary for peace. The headquarters of the organisation are in New York City. Ireland is a member.

The six principal organs of the UN are:

The General Assembly

This consists of all members of the United Nations. It normally meets in September each year and its session lasts until Christmas. The Assembly elects its own President for each session. Provisions exist for the holding of special and emergency sessions on specific problems as circumstances require. Each member-state has a single vote.

The General Assembly may discuss any matters of international concern, and make recommendations unless the issue is on the agenda of the Security Council. On important questions a two-thirds majority is necessary, on other matters a simple majority of members present and voting suffices. If the

Security Council fails to take action on a matter that threatens international peace, the General Assembly can make recommendations to its members on collective action.

The General Assembly disposes of its routine work through six main committees on which each member has the right to be represented. There are committees, for instance, to deal with political security issues, law, budgetary matters, economic and social affairs.

The General Assembly receives reports from other organs of the UN, including an annual report by the Secretary General on the work of the whole organisation.

In 1964 the UN Conference on Trade and Development, known as UNCTAD, was set up by resolution of the General Assembly as an organ charged with certain responsibilities in dealing with the problems of trade and aid facing the developing countries. UNCTAD's executive is known as the Trade and Development Board. It has fifty-five members and meets twice a year. The Board has set up four main committees to deal with Commodities, Manufactures, Invisibles and Financing, and Shipping.

The Security Council

The maintenance of peace and security — that is the main responsibility of the Security Council. It consists of fifteen members, each with one representative and one vote. China, France, USSR, Britain and USA are permanent members. The ten non-permanent members are elected for a two-year period by a two-thirds majority of the General Assembly. On all substantive questions, decisions are carried by nine affirmative votes if these include the concurring votes of all permanent members. (In practice, however, if a permanent member abstains it is not considered a veto.) Procedural matters are decided by any nine affirmative votes.

The Security Council functions continuously. For the maintenance of peace it can call on the armed forces and assistance of the member states.

Economic and Social Council

The functions of the UN in relation to international economic, social, cultural, educational, health and related matters are the responsibility of the Economic and Social Council. The Council consists of one delegate from each of fifty-four member states elected by the General Assembly for three year periods. The Council holds two sessions each year. It has a number of commissions and other organs of which, perhaps, the most important for Ireland is the Regional Economic Commission for Europe based in Geneva. All European countries are members of ECE. It in turn has a number of subsidiary committees dealing with such matters as trade development, transport, energy, agriculture, etc.

Trusteeship Council
This Council looks after the trusteeship system which operates to safeguard the interests of the inhabitants of some territories that are not yet fully self-governing.

International Court of Justice
This Court has its seat at The Hague. There are fifteen judges elected by the General Assembly and the Security Council. No two judges may be nationals of the same state. Judges are elected for a nine-year term. The Court is in permanent session except for judicial vacations.
Only States may be parties in cases before the Court.

Secretariat
The Secretariat consists of the Secretary-General and an international staff.

Specialised Agencies
The UN is associated with a number of specialised agencies, some of which, like UNESCO, are well-known.

UNESCO
The United Nations Educational, Scientific and Cultural Organisation was established in 1946. Its headquarters are in Paris. To promote education, UNESCO establishes regional and national training centres for teachers in under-developed areas of the world; to promote science it convenes international meetings of scientists, encourages research and aids the work of the international scientific organisations; to promote culture it

aims by research and advice to raise the standard of press, film and radio work throughout the world.

Ireland is a member of UNESCO.

World Health Organisation

The objective of WHO is to attain the highest possible level of health among people throughout the world. It carries out a large variety of functions — work aimed at eradicating disease, improving nutrition, housing, sanitation etc. At the request of governments it will provide technical assistance and, in emergencies, necessary aid. It promotes the study of health problems through conferences and publications.

Its headquarters are in Geneva. Ireland is a member of WHO.

Food and Agriculture Organisation

The FAO works to improve food production, processing and marketing and so achieve higher levels of nutrition and standard of living.

Its headquarters are in Rome. Ireland is a member of FAO.

International Labour Organisation

ILO aims to improve labour conditions, raise living standards and promote economic and social security. It is representative of governments, workers and employers. Its chief function is to formulate International Labour Conventions and Recommendations. Member countries submit Conventions to their appropriate national authorities for ratification and implementation. ILO also publishes material on labour relations.

Its headquarters are in Geneva. Ireland is a member of ILO.

World Bank

The World Bank or, as it is officially called, the International Bank for Reconstruction and Development, began operations in 1946 in Washington. The Bank loans money to member governments (of which there are 127). It loans out of money subscribed by members, funds raised by borrowings and its net earnings. The money borrowed is spent on such projects as electric power, agriculture, industry. The Bank also provides technical assistance. Ireland is a member.

International Development Association

To help poorer nations, the World Bank established, in 1960, the International Development Association which grants credit on a more flexible basis than the Bank itself for development projects. Ireland is a member.

International Finance Corporation

An affiliate of the World Bank, the IFC makes capital available to stimulate the growth of private enterprise in its less developed member countries and mobilises capital resources in other member countries for this purpose. There are 105 members of the IFC. Ireland is a member.

International Monetary Fund

The International Monetary Fund was established in 1945 in Washington. Its aim is to promote international monetary co-operation and exchange stability.

With the collaboration of member countries, it has established a pattern of fixed exchange rates. Changes by more than ten per cent in these rates must be approved by the Fund. Members may exchange limited amounts of their currencies for other currencies in the Fund in order to tide them over temporary deficits in their balance of payments. Ireland is a member.

General Agreement on Tariffs and Trade (GATT)

In 1946 the Economic and Social Council of the UN established a Committee to draft an international trade charter. This charter, known as the Havana Charter, was completed in 1948 but was not adopted when it became clear that it would not be ratified by the major powers. However, the member countries of the Committee concluded a General Agreement on Tariffs and Trade which came into force in 1948. By 1976, eighty-three countries were contracting parties to the Agreement and twenty-seven other countries were participating under various special arrangements.

GATT lays down a common code of conduct in international trade, provides machinery for reducing and stabilising tariffs and the opportunity for regular consultation on trade problems. GATT is flexible in applying its rules. Thus while it forbids the use of quantitative restrictions on imports in principle, this rule has been waived temporarily in the case of countries that have balance of payments difficulties.

The headquarters of GATT are in Geneva. GATT maintains close working relations with EEC and other regional groups. Ireland has acceded to GATT.

Universal Postal Union

Established in 1874, UPU aims to secure international collaboration for the improvement of the postal services, maintenance of the principle of liberty of transit for mail and the regulation of international postal charges.

Ireland became a separate member of UPU in 1922.

International Civil Aviation Organisation

Established in 1947, ICAO aims to promote the safe and orderly development of international civil aviation and the establishment of international standards and regulations.

Ireland became a member of ICAO in 1947.

International Telecommunications Union

Established in 1865, ITU aims to secure international co-operation for the improvement of telecommunications.

Ireland became a separate member of ITU in 1922.

World Meteorological Organisation

Established in 1947, WMO aims to secure international co-operation, standardisation and research in the field of meteorology generally, both theoretical and applied.

Ireland became a member of WMO in 1950.

Intergovernmental Maritime Consultative Organisation

Established in 1958, IMCO aims to secure international co-operation in maritime technical matters, improvement of the standards of safety and efficiency in navigation, removal of discrimination and restrictive practices affecting shipping.

Ireland became a member of IMCO in 1958.

International Atomic Energy Agency

Established in 1957, IAEA seeks to accelerate and enlarge

the contribution of atomic energy to peace, health and prosperity throughout the world. It assists research on and practical application of atomic energy for peaceful purposes.

IAEA has about 110 members. Ireland is a member.

Organisation for Economic Co-operation & Development

In 1961, OECD replaced OEEC (the Organisation for European Economic Co-operation) for, when Canada and the USA became full members, the OEEC had ceased to be purely European; furthermore it added development aid to its previous functions. Ireland is one of the twenty-five members of OECD. Its aims are to promote economic and social welfare in the member countries and to harmonise its members' aid efforts in favour of developing countries.

The *Council* of OECD is representative of all member countries. It meets at ministerial and official level. It is responsible for general policy and administration. It approves the budget, staff rules and regulations and senior staff appointments.

The *Executive Committee* is composed of representatives of thirteen member countries elected annually by the Council. All questions to be submitted to the Council are first examined by this committee which is responsible to the Council on all matters.

The OECD discharges its various functions through specialised committees. There are committees, for example, on development assistance, trade, agriculture and fisheries, tourism, manpower and social affairs.

The Council of Europe

The Council of Europe came into being in 1949 with the signature at London by ten countries (Belgium, Denmark, France, Ireland, Italy, Luxembourg, the Netherlands, Norway, Sweden and the United Kingdom) of the Statute of the Council of Europe. Eight other countries (Greece, Turkey, Iceland, Federal Republic of Germany, Malta, Austria, Cyprus and Switzerland) have since become members.

The Council's aim is to bring about greater unity among its members to safeguard and promote the ideals and principles which are their common heritage. The Council discusses issues of common concern, and makes agreements on economic, social, cultural, scientific, legal and administrative matters. National defence is outside its scope. Participation in the Council does not affect the collaboration of its members in the work of the UN and other international bodies.

The Council has its seat at Strasbourg. It has two main organs.

The Committee of Ministers

Each member nation nominates one representative, normally the Minister for Foreign Affairs, to the Committee. It meets twice yearly. Each country also appoints a Minister's Deputy, normally a senior civil servant. The deputies meet about once a month and have the same powers of decision as the Ministers themselves. The Committee of Ministers is the executive organ.

The Parliamentary Assembly

This consists of 154 parliamentarians appointed by national parliaments. Representation varies from three to eighteen. Ireland has four representatives.

Normally the Assembly meets three times a year. It works through specialised committees that make intensive studies of the questions submitted to them and prepare reports for consideration by the Assembly. Recommendations based on these reports are discussed by the Assembly and if agreed to are transmitted to the Council of Ministers for action on the international or domestic level.

The Council of Europe has been particularly active in drawing up international Conventions. Its Convention for the Protection of Human Rights and Fundamental Freedom brought into being the Commission and Court of Human Rights. The Council also provides a forum for the expression of European public opinion on major issues.

16. Conclusion

The War of Independence transferred the ruling power to the people of Ireland but it did not involve the radical social changes envisaged by a certain servant girl who threatened her Anglo-Irish mistress with the words: 'Youse'll be us and us'll be youse'. During the post-revolutionary turmoil, the state did not founder nor did government degenerate to autocracy. One of the main reasons for the stability of the state was the fact that many civil servants transferred their loyalty to the new regime and the governmental system inherited from the British allowed the new administration to exercise its authority effectively throughout the state. Moreover the system was geared to achieve democratic government: the franchise at both the local and parliamentary elections had been greatly extended (for instance in 1918 women of thirty years of age or over got the vote). Though the general antipathy towards Britain generated by the struggle for independence was not quickly dissipated, the main institutions of government employed by the British were adopted: the people were used to working them successfully and the principles on which they were based were acceptable. Of course, as the state developed changes were made to suit our circumstances. The public service has served our young state well. In the future the burden on the public service will increase — this is the experience of all modern states — and consequently there is now a pressing reason why the people of Ireland, on whom ultimately the responsibility for all state activity rests, must inform themselves more and more on the working of government, on what government can do and on what it cannot do.

The democratic interaction between government and governed allows the people to take a creative part in government and it conforms to a basic urge in man to control his own destiny. Thus one notable advantage democracy has over other forms of government is that it can generate a great amount of voluntary effort and co-operation for the common good. It is because we cannot afford to minimise one another's efforts on behalf of the community by lack of co-operation that democracy is crucial to our nation's welfare.

Appendix A
The Departments and Major Offices

The Department of Agriculture

The Department of Agriculture is charged with the implementation of government policy for the wellbeing, improvement and development of the country's agricultural industry.

The work of the department is aimed at helping our farmers to get the best possible return from their resources of land, labour and capital, to promote the efficient production of quality produce and to enable farmers to market their produce to the best possible advantage. The department operates various schemes and services designed to improve farm land, buildings, crops and livestock and the marketing of agricultural produce, including the development of market outlets at home and abroad. It provides educational and advisory facilities to farmers and conducts research on animal health, cereal breeding, etc. It administers a large volume of legislation dealing with product quality and crop and livestock disease control and eradication.

The Land Commission, which is attached to the department, consists of independent statutory Commissioners. It is responsible for the purchase and distribution of land for land structural reform purposes.

The Department of Defence

The Department of Defence is responsible for the administration generally of matters relating to the defence forces e.g. recruitment and training, organisation, regulation and control, purchase of stores and equipment, together with general planning, organisation and co-ordination of civil defence measures, including special guidance for local authorities. The department also administers various statutes regarding military pensions and allowances and controls the grant and issue of Service Medals. Other functions of the department include the administration of various lands, including the Curragh of Kildare, sea fishery protection, helicopter service and the provision of assistance to Cumann Croise Deirge na hÉireann (Irish Red Cross).

The Department of Economic Planning and Development

This department was established to promote and co-ordinate economic and social planning for the development of the economy both generally and as respects different sectors thereof and different regions of the country; identify the policies it considers necessary for general economic and social development and to report thereon to the government; identify in consultation with departments of state and to review and appraise the plans and activities of such departments giving effect to the policies for general economic and social development adopted by the government; make proposals to the government for the co-ordination of those plans and activities and for their integration with national economic and social plans; review the implementation of such national economic and social plans as may be approved by the government from time to time and to report thereon to the government. The department is at present organised in two major divisions as follows: (1) the Economic and Social Policy Division which deals with the formulation and development of national economic, sectoral and regional policies; (2) the Planning and Development Division which deals with the preparation and review of the plans and activities of departments of state giving effect to government policies for general economic and social development, integrating these plans and activities into national economic and social plans, and reporting on the national plans to the government.

The Department of Education

The Department of Education is responsible for the administration of public education in so far as the state is concerned. The department has under its survey, in varying degree, the education provided in primary, secondary, vocational, and special schools. The universities and their colleges are autonomous, but the department is the channel through which they receive their annual state subsidies. The National Museum of Ireland, the National Library, the National Gallery, the National College of Art and certain other institutions of a cultural nature, come within the administrative area of this department.

The Department of the Environment

The Department of the Environment is responsible for the overall structure of the local government system and for the co-ordination of the activities of local authorities. It is concerned with the constitution of local authorities, their area boundaries, local elections (and Dáil, Seanad, Presidential and European Parliament elections and referenda as well), the staffing and organisation of local authorities and the system of local finance and taxation. It is also responsible for the promotion and development of national policy in relation to many local services and activities — including physical planning and development, housing, water supply and sewerage schemes, road building and maintenance; it must therefore provide guidance and advice for local authorities in relation to these services. The department provides a number of public services directly: for example, it administers the national scheme of housing grants and the driver testing scheme; it also arranges for the provision of services for local authorities, including a system of combined purchasing of commodities required by them.

The Department of Finance

The Department of Finance has three Divisions:

(1) the Finance Division deals with raising and provision of money for state purposes, (other than by taxation); banking and credit; international trade and the European Communities.

(2) the Public Expenditure Division controls expenditure of individual departments and associated state-sponsored bodies.

(3) the Central Budget Division deals with budgetary policy; taxation; short-term economic forecasting and demand management.

The Minister for Finance is responsible to the Oireachtas for the Revenue Commissioners and the Office of Public Works.

The Department of Fisheries and Forestry

This department consists of two Divisions:

1. The Fisheries Division which promotes the development

of, and undertakes planning and co-ordinating activities in relation to sea and inland fisheries. It also channels funds to a number of other bodies concerned with such matters.

2. The Forest and Wildlife Service which is responsible for the development of afforestation with a view to providing as far as possible the country's requirements of timber and timber products. Its programme includes the management and development of state forests and the encouragement of private forestry. It is also responsible for the conservation and development of game and of wildlife (flora and fauna).

The Department of Foreign Affairs

The primary function of the Department of Foreign Affairs is to advise the government on Ireland's external relations and to act as the channel of official communication with foreign governments and international organisations.

The work of the Department of Foreign Affairs involves the collection through its diplomatic and consular representatives in foreign countries of information on all developments of interest to the Irish government in the political, economic, cultural or other fields and the presentation through the same representatives of Irish government policy in all such matters to the foreign governments concerned; the representation of Ireland at the United Nations and at other international organisations and conferences; the negotiation and ratification of international treaties and conventions; the development of Ireland's trade with other countries; the dissemination abroad of information on Ireland and the development of cultural relations with other countries; the granting of passports and visas and the protection of Irish citizens and their interests abroad; questions of international law; and matters concerning the diplomatic and consular representation of foreign countries in Ireland.

The Department of the Gaeltacht

The Department of the Gaeltacht promotes the cultural, social and economic welfare of the Gaeltacht and encourages the preservation of Irish.

The Department of Health

The Department of Health has overall control of the services provided by the health authorities throughout the country. In addition it reviews existing services and initiates proposals for new services.

The Department of Industry, Commerce and Energy

This Department is chiefly concerned with industrial development, the country's export trade in industrial products, legislation governing the incorporation and operations of business associations, the development of the country's mineral resources, price control, patents, trade marks and copyright and the formulation of national policies in relation to energy (which includes turf production, electricity, natural gas and nuclear power). The department is also responsible for certain state-sponsored bodies entrusted with the implementation of policy in regard to some of these functions, including the promotion of exports, the provision of grants for industrial projects and attracting external investment in Irish industry.

The Department of Justice

The Department of Justice administers the courts, prisons and police force in discharge of its primary function of preserving law and order and protecting the community against crime. It provides the Land Registry and Registry of Deeds for the registration of ownership to land and legal transactions affecting such ownership, and the Public Records Office which preserves documents of historic and scholarly interest. It is concerned, also, with charitable donations and bequests, censorship of films and publications, deeds of bravery, legal adoption, and has responsibility for aspects of law reform and certain legal publications as well as miscellaneous activities of the community connected with aliens, citizenship, firearms, explosives, fines, sentences, betting, lotteries, moneylending, pawnbroking, dance halls, intoxicating liquor licensing, street trading, landlord and tenant relations, rent control, coroners and peace commissioners.

The Department of Labour

This department is responsible for legislation relating to the

occupational safety, health and welfare of workers and to conditions of employment. The inspectors of the department
advise employers how to comply with that legislation and
ensure that workers have the protection to which they are
legally entitled. The department is also responsible for
industrial relations and trade union law and for industrial relations generally. It is responsible for manpower policy, including the training and re-training of workers, the collection
of information on the labour market, forecasting manpower
requirements and the operation of placement and guidance
functions through its National Manpower Service. The operation of schemes of redundancy payments and resettlement
allowances and of the employment incentive and maintenance
schemes is another responsibility of the department. The
department engages in the promotion of the standards set by
the Conventions and Recommendations of the International
Labour Organisation. The Department of Labour also for-
mulates and transmits to the EEC Commission applications for
assistance from the European Social Fund towards the costs of
training, retraining and resettlement of workers.

The Department of Posts and Telegraphs
    The Department of Posts and Telegraphs is responsible for
the operation of the public postal, telephone and telegraph services of the state, and, in addition, operates such services as the
Post Office Savings Bank and Savings Certificates. The department also purchases engineering stores and uniforms for itself
and for the government service generally, undertakes payment
— through its 2,200 Head and Sub-Post Offices throughout
the country — of old age pension and other social welfare
benefits, and co-operates with the Department of Tourism and
Transport in the provision of certain civil aviation services.
The Minister for Posts and Telegraphs has certain functions in
relation to Radio Telefís Éireann under the Broadcasting
Authority Acts.

The Department of the Public Service
    The report of the Public Service Organisation Review Group
(the Devlin Report) recommended that a new department
should be set up to deal with public service organisation and

personnel matters (including remuneration). In 1973 this department was established by the government and charged with the reorganisation of the public service on the lines recommended by Devlin.

The Office of Public Works
The Office of Public Works is responsible for providing office accommodation for government services (including diplomatic missions abroad) and for the building of new primary schools, Garda stations and important post offices. It also undertakes large-scale arterial drainage works and marine engineering works such as major improvements of fishery harbours. It manages state harbours and certain public parks. The office issues loans to local authorities from the Local Loans Fund and collects repayments. It is also entrusted with the care and preservation of national monuments.

The Revenue Commissioners
The Revenue Commissioners, who are responsible to the Minister for Finance, are responsible for the collection and administration of virtually all taxes and duties, including customs and excise duties, income tax, value added tax (VAT) and stamp duties. Their office also undertakes a considerable volume of non-revenue work on behalf of other departments (such as the enforcement of import and export controls, the compilation of statistics relating to imports and exports of dutiable goods, the printing of postage stamps and postal orders). In addition, the Revenue Commissioners play an important role in advising the Minister for Finance on budgetary and other problems relating to the taxes and duties for which they are responsible.

The Department of Social Welfare
The Department of Social Welfare is responsible for the administration of the state social security schemes established by the Social Welfare and other similar Acts. These, which comprise insurance and assistance schemes, provide for regular cash payments to qualified unemployed and sick persons, old persons, the blind, widows and orphans, as well as payments on marriage and maternity and to families with young

children. A scheme of occupational injuries insurance which provides cover against occupational accidents and diseases is also administered by the department.

The Department of the Taoiseach

This department acts as the secretariat to the government and is concerned also with the carrying out by the Taoiseach of his functions under the Constitution and under statute. It has the custody of the Public Archives and is responsible for the administration of such of the public services as are not assigned to any other department. It is also the channel of communication between government departments and the President. The Government Information Services are attached to this department as is the Office of the Minister of State to the Taoiseach, which is concerned mainly with the co-ordination of the government's programme of legislative and other business in the Houses of the Oireachtas.

The Department of Tourism and Transport

This department is responsible for the formulation of national policies connected with tourism, aviation, shipping and rail and road transport. The state-sponsored bodies under the aegis of the department are charged with the implementation of these policies.

The department is also responsible for the construction of airports and also operates meteorological, telecommunications and air traffic control services providing essential aids to air navigation.

Appendix B
The Land

The State shall, in particular, direct its policy towards securing . . . that there may be established on the land in economic security as many families as in the circumstances shall be practicable.

The Irish land problem had its roots in the plantations and confiscations of the sixteenth and seventeenth centuries when the ownership of the land was transferred to a Protestant minority, the bulk of the people becoming tenants. Uncertainty of tenure remained a great grievance right down to the end of the nineteenth century.

Absentee landlordism aggravated the problem not only because most of the money collected in rents was spent abroad but also because the management of estates was left in the hands of agents, paid on results, or let to middle men.

Moreover, the conditions of the late eighteenth and early nineteenth centuries encouraged the excessive sub-division of holdings as well as progressive increases in the number of tenants. The political system gave considerable power to the landlord who had a large number of tenants, the Napoleonic Wars made tillage profitable and the potato yielded an extremely cheap staple food for tenants farming a small area.

The immediate cause of the repeal of the Corn Laws in 1846, the second year of the Famine, was the need to allow the importation of cheap, foreign cereals into Ireland. The ending of the war, however, had made tillage less profitable and so landlords had begun to make 'clearances' of their estates — by wholesale eviction and consolidation of holdings — to engage in the now profitable business of rearing cattle. The Land Act of 1860 (Deasy's Act) accelerated this process for it simplified and increased the remedies of the landlord for recovering possession of the land and rendered more drastic the law of ejectment for non-payment of rent and on notice to quit. The chief results of these clearances were large-scale emigration, bloodshed and boycott, and even greater congestion in the poorer areas.

The writing on the wall for Irish landlordism came with the appearance in politics of Parnell and Davitt. In 1879 Davitt founded the Irish Land League and thereby inaugurated a movement that at last gave the cause of the Irish tenant shape and aim. The two leaders found themselves in control of a vast human machine that carried out orders such as the boycott of the League's enemies and the withholding of rent payments, etc. The great Land War of the 70s and 80s of the last century was the immediate cause of the passing of the remarkable body of legislation, known as the Irish Land Code, that has achieved in eighty years a veritable revolution on Irish land, supplanting the landlords by the people as full proprietors of their farms and holdings.

The Land Acts

Land Act, 1870

This Act attempted to ensure that tenants should be compensated for disturbances and improvements. It failed because it was adversely interpreted by unsympathetic courts.

Land (Gladstone) Act, 1881

This Act broke the landlords' absolute control of their estates. It legalised what were called the 'Three Fs' — *fixity of tenure* for the tenant so long as he paid his rent and observed his covenants, *fair rent,* fixed by an independent tribunal, and *free sale* by the tenant of his interest in his holding.

This Act set up the Irish Land Commission to fix fair rents (subject to possible further revision after 15 years) at the request of landlord or tenant. The effect of the Land Commission's work was to reduce rents (in a great number of cases by up to 21 per cent). These revised rents formed the basis of purchase annuities in respect of judicial holdings vested in tenant purchasers under the later Land Acts.

The Act also empowered the Land Commission to make advances to tenants for the purchase of their holdings and enabled it to purchase land for resale to the tenants. These purchase provisions were utilised to a very small extent only because few tenants could make the initial down payment, and the short term of repayment involved a high rate of annuity.

Later Land Acts

Since it established the tenants' rights the Gladstone Act was indeed progressive. However, it was not radical enough. It began to dawn on all the political parties — Conservatives, Liberals and Nationalists — that the ultimate remedy was to abolish landlordism and replace it with a system of tenant-proprietorship. The later Land Acts aimed at providing loans to the tenants on increasingly favourable terms to buy out their holdings. Initially the Government provided the loan money; then under the Balfour Act, 1891, the landlord was paid not in cash but in Land Stock. (This Act also established the Congested Districts Board to deal with the problem of congestion in the poorer western areas.) The Wyndham Act, 1903, introduced the idea of the state bridging the gap between what the tenant was willing to pay and the landlord willing to accept and by tying the payment of the bonus to the sale of estates in their entirety the Act gave the tenant the opportunity not only of buying out his holding but also of enlarging it to make it economic. The Birrell Act, 1909, brought a further improvement in the financing of land purchase and introduced a significant change in principle — it gave the Land Commission and the Congested Districts Board power to acquire land compulsorily to relieve congestion.

Effects of British Legislation

Over 316,000 holdings comprising an area of over 11,000,000 acres were purchased for some £100,000,000. In addition 750,000 acres of untenanted land had been distributed amongst 35,000 allottees, to make holdings economic and to create some new ones. (Of this total 600,000 acres were distributed within the congested counties — Donegal, Sligo, Leitrim, Roscommon, Mayo, Galway, Kerry and parts of Clare and Cork.)

Native legislation

The agrarian problem facing the native government was still very complex — the transfer of 110,000 holdings comprising over 3,000,000 acres to the full ownership of the respective tenants and the acquisition for the relief of congestion of almost 2,000,000 acres.

Land Act, 1923

This Act made compulsory the sale of land to tenants and the acquisition of land to relieve congestion. The Congested Districts Board had been abolished and control of the machinery for land settlement was unified in the hands of the Land Commission. The Act gave power to complete the creation of a tenant proprietorship and helped further to eliminate uneconomic holdings particularly in the West. It also made provision to control the subdivision of holdings by proprietors so that no more uneconomic holdings would be made.

Compensation to landlords, which was payable in 4½ per cent Land Bonds, became automatic under the Act. Known as the standard price, this payment represented a sum the interest on which at 4¾ per cent was to be equal to the new standard purchase annuity which, in turn, was to equate to a reduction of 35 per cent or 30 per cent in judicial rents fixed earlier, depending on the date of such fixation.

Later Land Acts

The later Land Acts aimed at speeding up the scheme of settlement by enlarging the powers of the Land Commission and reducing purchase annuities.

The result of the Land Acts has been to abolish landlordism, without recourse to confiscation, and to establish a wide distribution of property within the state. Some 400,000 tenants-at-will and their successors have been transformed into owners in fee simple.

The Land Commission

Since 1923 the Land Commission has had full responsibility for the administration of the Land Code. It consists of a Judicial Commissioner (who must be a judge of the High Court) and four Lay Commissioners who are appointed by the government and who hold their positions under rules similar to those affecting judges. The Commission is part of the Department of Agriculture and in matters of general policy and administration it is subject to the Minister for Agriculture but in relation to land purchase and land settlement operations affecting individual citizens, the Commissioners have independent jurisdiction subject only to the right of appeal to the Judicial Commissioner and the Supreme Court, chiefly on questions of law. The Judicial Commissioner has final jurisdiction on questions of value; he also deals with the allocation of purchase moneys to landlords and claimants. Amongst other matters, the Commissioners have sole power to determine:

(1) the persons from whom land is to be acquired
(2) the actual lands to be acquired
(3) the price to be paid
(4) the persons to whom (and the price at which) the land shall be allotted, etc.

In granting wide powers of acquisition to the Land Commission the legislature imposed limitations in order to prevent the possibility of injustice and to preserve, as far as possible, consistent with the safety and well-being of the community, the rights and freedom of the individual citizen. The legal process of acquiring land, then, is a lengthy one and the Commissioners must personally consider each individual case and give their decision with strict impartiality and justice.

Apart from acquiring and vesting land and re-structuring holdings, the Land Commission has arranged for the migration of families from congested areas. Moreover before selling land to tenant purchasers and allottees, the Land Commission carries out necessary improvements, such as providing roads, fences, drainage, dwelling houses, outoffices, etc.

The staff of the Land Commission is composed of full-time civil servants.

Appendix C
The Irish Language

Up to the 19th century most of the Irish people spoke, as they had done from time immemorial, the Irish language. Due to a combination of economic, political, social and cultural forces in the 19th century the decline of the language became catastrophic. The massive emigration that followed the Famine not only reduced drastically the Irish-speaking population, it encouraged the view that English would be a more useful language for the potential emigrants of the future. The National School system provided a means for the diffusion of English throughout the country. English, as the official language, was needed by those who wished to advance in the public service, in the arts, the professions, politics. Irish came to be looked upon as a badge of ignorance and poverty, the more especially as some of the national leaders abandoned its use. Within a few generations Irish ceased to be widely used as a spoken language outside certain western and southern districts known as the Gaeltacht. And even in these districts the population steadily declined to only 70,568 according to the 1971 census.

Gaelic League

The Gaelic League was founded in 1893 to preserve Irish as the national language of Ireland and to spread its use as a spoken language. Earlier a number of other organisations interested in preserving the language had been set up and had made progress. Most of these, however, concentrated on literature and had not found it necessary to concern themselves about the spoken language. The efforts of the Gaelic League to preserve and spread the spoken language were spectacularly successful and by the early years of the present century, it had 600 branches scattered throughout the country where thousands studied the rudiments of the language and learned the history, songs and dances of Ireland. A chain of Irish Summer Colleges was established in the Gaeltacht. Teachers and pupils attending these improved their knowledge by contact with the living speech. Feiseanna had become a popular feature of the Summer months and the Oireachtas had been inaugurated as an annual Gaelic festival.

The League successfully organised public opinion to demand a higher status for Irish in the educational system. By the end of the British administration in 1921 the number of schools in which Irish was taught had risen to almost a quarter of the total. The teaching of Irish was expanded also in the secondary schools where it was given a strong impetus by the inclusion of Irish among the subjects necessary for matriculation in the National University.

The Gaelic League also advanced the cause of Irish writing by the publication of old and new literature. The League worked to inculcate in the people a strong sense of self-reliance in the economic, cultural and political spheres and this spirit permeated the whole national movement so that the crusade to restore the language went hand in hand with the struggle for political independence. Indeed it was through the Gaelic League that many of those who later became national leaders first became interested in Irish national affairs.

Under native government

With the foundation of Saorstát Éireann in 1922 the language acquired official status. Its revival as a spoken language throughout the country became state policy. State servants were henceforth expected to have a knowledge of Irish. Irish was given a high place in the curricula of the schools. Ever since 1922 special steps have been taken to preserve the Gaeltacht. In 1956 a separate Department, Roinn na Gaeltachta, was set up to foster the cultural, social and economic development of the Gaeltacht. Publication of books and periodicals in Irish has been stepped up. Irish has its place in the national radio and television services. Some film-making has been done in Irish. The written language has been standardised. Technical terms and reference books have been provided.

In 1978 a new state-sponsored body called Bord na Gaeilge was established. Its function is to promote the Irish language, particularly its use as a living language and a general medium of communication. It has wide powers to carry out its functions.

In addition to the state, numerous voluntary organisations

are engaged in the work of revival, their efforts being co-ordinated by *Comhdháil Náisiúnta na Gaeilge.*

Despite state and voluntary efforts and although at least one-fifth of the people may be classed as Irish speakers, the language revival has not yet made a real break-through.

Appendix D
The National Flag

There does not appear to be any record of the tricolour as an Irish national flag prior to 1848. In that year, on the return of Mr William Smith O'Brien and others who had formed a deputation to France, a public entertainment was organised for them. The following is an account:

"Thomas Francis Meagher, in reply to the toast 'Messrs Meagher, O'Gorman and Hollywood and the remainder of the deputation to France,' referred to the freedom enjoyed by Republican France, and formally presented to the Chairman the flag surmounted by the Irish pike. The material was of the richest French silk, which was most gorgeously trimmed and embroidered; the colours were orange, white and green. As the Chairman took the flag, the whole company stood up and cheered most enthusiastically. Mr Meagher resumed — 'From Paris, the gay and gallant city of the tricolour and the barricade, this flag has been proudly borne. I present it to my native land and I trust that the old country will not refuse this symbol of a new life from one of her youngest children. I need not explain its meaning. The quick and passionate intellect of the generation now springing into arms will catch it at a glance. The white in the centre signifies a lasting truce between the 'Orange' and the 'Green', and I trust that beneath its folds the hands of the Irish Protestant and the Irish Catholic may be clasped in generous and heroic brotherhood. If this flag be destined to fan the flame of war, let England behold once more, upon that white centre, the Red Hand that struck her down from the hills of Ulster, and I pray that Heaven may bless the vengeance it is sure to kindle.'

Following Meagher came Mitchel, who delivered his famous 'plain as a pike staff' speech, in which he concludes with — 'Ah, the gleaming pikehead rises through our darkness like a morning star. This magnificent Irish tricolour, with its orange, white and green, dawns upon us more gloriously than ever sunburst flashed over the field of Benburb, or blazed through the battle haze of Clontarf. My friends, I hope to see that flag one

day waving as our national banner over a forest of Irish
pikes . . . '"

> —*Memoirs of General Thomas Francis
> Meagher,* by Michael Cavanagh.

It is evident that the tricolour, although the idea of Meagher
was, in fact, a scheme of Mitchel, O'Gorman and the remaining members of the Paris deputation.

We find no further instance of the tricolour being introduced into any national emblem until we meet the orange,
white and green in the Sinn Féin postage stamp (about 1908).
This stamp was used solely as a means of Sinn Féin
propaganda. It is of importance, however, because it shows
that Griffith, as early as 1908, had accepted Meagher's colours.

In an article published in the *Irish Volunteer* (May 1914),
The O'Rahilly advocated the adoption of Company flags in
conjunction with the adoption of a general national flag, the
national flag being the old green one with the golden harp in
the centre. Pearse adopted the tricolour as the Company flag
of 'E' Company, 4th Battalion, Dublin, and when this Company entered the G.P.O. on 24 April 1916, they hoisted the
green, white and orange tricolour on the flagstaff.

During the period 1914-16, it was fashionable to wear
favours, such as rosettes, ribbons, buttons, etc., on every
public occasion and the tricolour was adopted by the followers
of Sinn Féin; hence they came to be popularly known as the
Sinn Féin colours. Indeed, the colours were publicly displayed
for the first time on the occasion of the lying-in-state and
burial of O'Donovan Rossa in August 1914.

At this time, little was known as to the origin and subsequent
history of the Sinn Féin flag, for we find in *Nationality* (26 May
1917) a notice (probably written by Griffith): 'The green, white
and orange flag which is variously described as the Sinn Féin or
'Republican' flag, is the flag of the Young Irelanders, adopted
70 years ago, and by them avowed as a symbol of the Union of
Ireland against enforced union with England'. The tricolour
was not adopted by the extreme wing of the labour movement
before April, 1916, since Connolly, shortly before the Rising,
at a parade of the Citizen Army, publicly unfurled the green
flag, bearing a harp without a crown, from the flagstaff of

Liberty Hall on Sunday 16 April (*Irish Times*, 17 April 1916).

The colour scheme adopted by Meagher, according to Michael Cavanagh's *Memoirs of General Meagher,* was orange, white and green, whereas the present arrangement is green, white and orange..

The Irish tricolour is essentially a flag of union. It stands for the fusion of the Irish and Norman-Irish elements, represented by the green, with the newer Protestant stock which produced Grattan, Emmet, Mitchel and Tone. The adoption of the orange to denote the latter dates from the Williamite Wars, when the bulk of their number took the side of William of Orange.

The tricolour is recognised as the National Flag by the Constitution.

Design and Display

The flag should be rectangular in shape, the width being twice its depth. The flag should normally be displayed on a staff, the green being next to the staff.

Appendix E
The National Anthem

Like the splendid *Marseillaise*, the Irish national anthem, Amhrán na bhFiann (in English 'The Soldier's Song'), was initially a rousing revolutionary song. The words were written in 1907 by Peadar Kearney, a poet, songster and soldier, and an uncle of playwright Brendan Behan. The music was composed by Kearney's friend, Patrick Heeney, in association with Kearney himself. The song got a cold reception in the National clubs at first but gradually the air caught on. Bulmer Hobson published the song in *Irish Freedom* in 1912. The Irish Volunteers adopted the song and after Easter Week 1916 it was sung in the internment camps. It became the *de facto* national anthem, superseding the Fenian anthem, *God Save Ireland*. In May 1924, the Soldier's Song was informally adopted as the national anthem. In July 1926 the Executive Council of the Irish Free State ruled that it alone should be recognised as the national anthem at home and abroad. A week later this ruling was formally announced in the Dáil in answer to a Deputy's question.

Index

149

Public Service Advisory Council 43
Public Services Organisation Review
   Group (Devlin Committee) 41-43,
   53, 73, 80, 81, 82, 134-135

Radio Telefis Eireann 80, 134
rates 53, 57, 59, 67, 68, 69
regional: development organisations 55,
   58; health boards 39, 53, 54, 55,
   57-58, 68; hospital boards 58; technica
   colleges 59; tourism organisations 58,
   78
register of local electors 55
Revenue Commissioners 35, 131, 135
roads 53, 54, 60, 61, 62-63, 69, 71,
   72, 131 *see also* traffic

sanitary services 64, 68-69
select committee 23
Senate (An Seanad) 5, 7, 10, 11,
   13-27, 28, 29, 30, 38, 131; attendance
   in 19-20; Cathaoirleach 11, 20, 26-27;
   clerk of 19, 27; leader of 22; Leas-
   Cathaoirleach 20; membership of
   19-21; panels of candidates 20
senators 20, 25, 26, 27, 38
sewerage 60, 61, 64, 68, 69, 131
Slua Muiri, An, 103, 106
Social Welfare, Dept of, 35, 135-136
solicitors 90, 91, 94-95, 96-97
special committee 23
stamp duties 50, 135
state-sponsored bodies 13, 25-26, 32,
   37, 39, 42, 50, 51, 52, 70, 71-83, 131,
   133, 136, 143
statutory instruments 23

Tanaiste 11, 20, 28, 30
Taoiseach 7, 10, 11, 13, 20, 26, 28,
   29-31, 34, 93, 136; Dept of 34,

35, 39, 131, 136; Office of Minister
   of State to 136
taxation: state 24, 33, 47, 50-51, 52,
   135; local authority 67
Teachtai Dala (TDs) 13, 20, 25, 26, 27,
   38
Tourism and Transport: Dept of 35, 134,
   136; Minister for 76
Town: Commissions 53, 56-57;
   Commissioners 64, 66, 67, 69
traffic, road, 23, 54, 60, 61, 62,
   63, 99 *see also* road
Trinity College 12, 13, 20

Ulster 5
United Nations 109, 119-125, 132
University of Dublin (Trinity College) 12,
   13, 20
urban district councils 54, 56-57, 58, 60,
   61, 66, 68, 69
urban renewal 61, 62

Valuation Office 35
value added tax 50, 135
Vocational Education Committee,
   County, 54, 55, 58-59, 68
vocational schools 59, 68, 130
Voluntary Health Insurance Board 80
voted capital services 50

waste disposal 64
water suply 60, 61, 64, 68, 69, 72,
   131
Weights and Measures 66, 99
Westminster 5, 6, 110-111
World Bank 122
World Health Organisation (WHO) 122
World Meteorological Organisation
   (WMO) 124